Mechanics of Starting a Home-Based Business

Second Edition

Nancy Miller
and
Mike Rounds

CPM Systems ❧ Rancho Palos Verdes, California, USA

Mechanics of Starting a Home-Based Business
Second Edition
by Nancy Miller and Mike Rounds

Published by:

PUBLISHING COMPANY
6318 Ridgepath Court
Rancho Palos Verdes, CA 90275-3248
CPMSystems@RoundsMiller.com

This edition is an expansion and revision of a work previously published as *Mechanics of Mail Order* copyright © 1992, 1993, 1995, 1996, 2003 by Nancy Miller and Michael F. Rounds published by CPM Systems.

Cartoons by Brad Veley 906-228-3229 brad@bradveley.com

Library of Congress Cataloging-in-Publication Data

Miller, Nancy, 1958-
  Mechanics of starting a home-based business / Nancy Miller and Mike Rounds.
    p. cm.
  Expanded and rev. ed. of: Mechanics of mail-order . 2nd ed. rev. c2003.
  Includes bibliographical references.
  ISBN 1-891440-20-9
  1. Mail-order business. 2. Home-based businesses. I. Rounds, Mike. II. Title.

  HF5466.M43 2007
  658.1'1412--dc22

2007008556

Table of Contents

Bob's home-based business was unique for a number of reasons, the most obvious being that it wasn't even his home.

CHAPTER 1 WELCOME TO YOUR BUSINESS

America's work force went home and stayed there!

A home-based business is a business whose primary office is in the owner's home. The business can be any size or any type as long as the office itself is located in a home. Increasingly, people use their homes to earn a primary income, not a secondary or supplementary income.

> *"68 percent of all new business start-up ventures are single person, home-based businesses."*
> *an article*

According to the Small Business Administration, today more than half (53 percent) of the small businesses in the US are home-based. In brute numbers, that's more than 24 million. As of 2005, in North America alone, as many as one million people enjoyed the freedom and benefits of owning their own Internet business.

Entrepreneur magazine estimates that $427 billion is generated each year by home-based businesses. That's bigger than General Motors, Ford, and Chrysler all put together.

How is this possible? The extremely low start-up costs, flexible hours, and the Internet are all fueling the growth of the home business segment.

Hundreds of thousands of individuals decide to start a home-based business each year, and many of them succeed. About 70 percent of home-based businesses will last over a three-year period, compared to 29 percent of other business ventures, according to the Home-Based Business Institute.

"Many entrepreneurs start firms from their homes and stay there," states a November 2000 report from the **Small Business Administration's** (www.SBA.gov) Office of Advocacy. "This year, nearly 20,000 entrepreneurs grossed more than $1 million operating from a home-based environment."

The Small Business Administration is a government program. Although many people think that this is a good place to go to for assistance in starting their home-based business. So what size of business does the SBA typically serve? It's not all that small.

- 500 employees for most manufacturing and mining industries

- 100 employees for all wholesale trade industries

- $7.0 million for most retail and service industries

- $33.5 million for most general and heavy construction industries

- $14.0 million for all special trade contractors

- $750,000 for most agricultural industries

Although the government is helping small businesses, the primary focus is not on mom and pop operations. In fact, the small businesses that received the most Small Business **loans** were Super 8 and Burger King. If you are looking at obtaining a loan with the SBA, do you qualify for a loan at your local bank? If so, you may qualify for a loan with the SBA. This is a loan, not free money. The SBA wants repayment. Also they typically may not loan you 100 percent of what you are asking. They want you to come up with perhaps 10 percent yourself.

For the truly small guys, the SBA has a program called the **SBDC** (Small Business Development Center). They provide classes and seminars for small businesses—from birth to death of the business. SBDC program is free, but the seminars may have a fee to attend.

A good seminar to take would be a business plan seminar. For a small guy's business plan, focus on the next 12 to 18 months. Many times business plans focus on 5-years, 10-years, and 20-years projections. Although those goals are good for a larger business, for a home-based business, focusing on the first year and then the second is more realistic.

Before starting a start-up, home-based, mail order or Internet business, entrepreneurs should consider several key questions:

- Can you operate the business with little or no help?

- How does your family feel about you working for yourself from the same home they occupy?

- Do you have contact with clients for your services?

- Can distributors, sales staff, clients and others reach your business without difficulty?

- Is start-up and operations capital available for the first year?

- Can the business be operated from your home?

- Do you have separate spaces for storage, records and parking?

- Can a business in the home compete with similar businesses?

As with most businesses, there are advantages and disadvantages to a start-up, home-based, mail order and Internet business.

A business in the home permits flexibility of working hours and lower start-up costs, and it allows family affairs to continue during business hours. The average home-based business requires about $10,000 in start-up costs. Although this may be much less than the cost of opening a business outside the home, both the start-up and operating funds should be in hand before beginning the business operation.

Modern communications help to alleviate the problem of being isolated from your vendors, clients, or customers. Internet access is almost certainly necessary for communications within the business community.

"I'm my own boss." Sounds pretty good, doesn't it? No wonder so many Americans start businesses every year. Entrepreneurship provides an ideal opportunity to take control of your career, set your own schedule and pursue long-held interests or new opportunities.

There are also disadvantages—zoning restrictions in your residential community may prohibit a home-based, mail order or Internet business, it may be difficult to get materials and customers to your home or financing the business could be challenging.

Starting a business requires hard work and relentless motivation. So, before you dive into this life-changing decision, make sure you are ready. The **SCORE** (Service Corps Of Retired Executives) (www.SCORE.org) division of the **SBA** has developed the following quiz to determine if you have got what it takes to be your own boss.

- Can you work irregular, long hours and weekends to make a great start?

- Do you have enough capital to support you and your business through the start-up phase?

- Are you passionate about the business you are thinking of starting?

- Do you have outside support from an advisor or mentor with business expertise?

- Have you studied the demand for your business and calculated the sales potential?

Any *no* answers are areas of risk and potential problems that need to be addressed before you embark on your own business venture.

GOLDEN RULES FOR A START-UP BUSINESS

We want you to succeed. In our numerous years of business, we have observed successful businesses, worked in successful businesses, worked in unsuccessful businesses, and watched good businesses fail. As a result, we have created four rules to help you succeed.

Rule #1: When spending your money, ask yourself if that expenditure will make a difference between the customer ordering and not ordering.

We have had some great examples of companies not adhering to this rule (dot com companies). They received millions of dollars in venture capital. That money was often spent on high salaries, extravagant release parties, and expensive office furniture. The customers didn't care about any of those things. They wanted a product that worked.

There are a great series of books by Jeff Slutsky called *Street Smart Marketing* to help overcome the disadvantages of being small. The premise of the book is that a small company can swiftly make changes compared to a large business. As the book is older, you may be able to only find them at a library.

Rule #2: Speed costs, so ask yourself how fast do you want to go.

Getting your customers' money faster costs money. If you want to operate your business with 24-hour operators, it will cost you money, but it will increase orders. As a start-up business, adding those extras costs frequently means money out of your pocket. How fast do you need to go?

The old adage says: *it takes money to make money* applies. As a business, this money comes from two places—your pocket (keep it there for emergencies) and customer sales. Cash flow will keep you healthy.

Rule #3: There are two places to invest your money in business. They are: product and advertising. Of these two, **advertising is more important.**

You need a product or service to sell. Specifically, with products, you do not need to have a whole warehouse full before you begin selling it. Start small and build up your inventory. Concentrate on advertising.

Get the customers' money first, and then solve the problem. If you solve the problem first, customers may never part with their money (purchase your product). If you can't solve the problem, you can always refund the money.

Rule #4: Use conventional advertising to drive people to your Web site.

People feel that if they build a Web site, customers will come—just show up. The truth is that although it is easier for people to find Web sites compared to driving up and down streets looking for a storefront it still not all that easy to find you.

A business must still advertise, whether that means using newspapers, magazines, radio, direct mail or someone standing on a street corner twirling a sign. Don't depend on search engines to do your work. Yes, search engines will eventually list you, but will the customers know what words to use to find you? Use your Web site as your four-color catalog. A Web site is best used for anything you would have to print (catalog, sell sheets, and photographs).

That's it. Four basic and simple rules for the start-up, home-based, mail order, and Internet business. By putting them into practice, your chances for success will increase.

There are programs on television that might be of interest to you and help you gain additional insight about starting a business.

The Big Idea with Donny Deutsch on CNBC (one hour, five days a week). Donny Deutsch interviews a variety of people. Usually the individual is someone who has recently become a successful business. There are also interviews with people who are just beginning their business. The guest's backgrounds come from a variety of sources such as marketing, finance, and management so there is a broad view of business. This was cancelled but you can watch it on-line in streaming video.

Dragon's Den on BBCAmerica (one hour) is where entrepreneurs pitch for investment, five venture capitalists willing to invest their own money in exchange for equity. This program is for entertainment, and therefore has been edited for entertainment value. There have been times when we wished that they had more of the business discussion rather than the drama in an episode. However, Dragon's Den can give you insight into what it would take to advance your company to the next level. There is an American version called **Shark Tank** on ABC.

Introduction to Entrepreneurship: Building the Dream (check your local listing) this is a short series of 12 episodes that is repeated by Thomas O'Malia, Director of the Entrepreneurship Program at the University of Southern California. The series is older and sometimes boring. But I find that I keep quoting the dude! The information is correct. The stories (video clips) are very interesting.

If you are interested in more information on this topic, you may want to purchase Venture Capital for the Clueless®. Details are available in the back of this book.

The Pitchmen on The Discovery Channel (13-episode of one hour) with pitchmen Billy Mays and Anthony Sullivan. The show follows the pitch by the inventor to the results of the 2-minute infomercial and all the turmoil in between. Watching all episodes will give you insight into pricing, trademark issues, the WOW factor and much more. Very informative and entertaining. Available in DVD.

To gain further insight, and to be able to talk to people about their business, you may want to join other organizations that are directly relevant to what you sell and what you do as a start-up, home-based, mail order and Internet business. The National Association of the Self-Employed (NASE) (www.NASE.org) can provide help and information as well as the Chamber of Commerce. Leads Club (www.LeadsClub.com) or Le Tip (www.LeTip.com) are leads clubs.

You also may want to check out **NARMS** (National Association for Retail Marketing Services). Nancy's brother told her about the association. He has a friend who is making a living from work provided by NARMS (www.NARMS.com).

RIGHT TIME TO START A BUSINESS

Think that now is a bad time to start a home-based, mail order or Internet business because of the economy? During the times of downturns the following business were started and are still in business today. Perhaps you have heard of them: FedEx, General Electric, General Motors, IBM, Procter & Gamble, and United Technologies Corp.

The story about FedEx's beginning is interesting. While attending Yale, Fred Smith wrote a paper for an economics class, outlining overnight delivery service in a computer information age. Folklore suggests he received a C for this paper although in a later interview he claims that when asked he told a reporter "I don't know what grade, probably made my usual C". The paper became the idea of FedEx (for years, the sample package displayed in the company's print advertisements featured a return address at Yale). FedEx began operations on April 17, 1973.

The marketing Rule of Seven has its origins in the motion picture industry in the depression where movie moguls learned that it took seven messages to get people in front of their silver screens.

What was discovered was that just one exposure to a movie wouldn't make a person go to the movie. They had to be exposed to that movie seven times before they acted (bought a movie ticket).

This rule is still in evidence today. If you receive a catalog with a sticker say: this is your last catalog unless you order! They have sent you six catalogs and you haven't ordered.

WHAT IS A HOME-BASED COMPUTER BUSINESS

> *"A computer is a purposeless device with universal application."*
> *Mike Rounds*

First of all, what is your definition of a home-based business?

1. Is it a business where when you wake up in the morning you walk to your office, sit at the computer. Then, at day's end, walk back to your bedroom, never leaving the house all day?

2. Is it the administrative part of the business where you have your office/desk in the home and go out to client's locations to do the business?

   Both of these are home-based businesses.

3. Are you going to be selling a product or service? Either can be a home-based business.

4. What is your expectation of income?

   a. Do you want to make enough money to pay for your mortgage and life-style each month?

   > *"An entrepreneur is someone who will work 80 hours a week for themselves so that they don't have to work 40 hours a week for someone else."*

   b. Do you want just a part-time job with part-time income? Do you want some additional pocket money?

Although the products and services in this book may provide an income, it may be more effort than you are willing to provide or not enough income for your needs.

You have just taken the first and hardest step of creating a business using your computer. Because the computer is that purposeless device that opens the universe to you, what do you want to do with it? This book is not a get rich scheme, nor are we trying to convince you that one type of business is better than another. You will need to decide that for yourself.

What we will help you with is some brain storming and becoming a resource guide where you can find legitimate answers.

Your **local library is** a great resource. Check out books on home-based businesses and also on specific subject matter. There are books on the business of sewing; selling on eBay; how to start a home-based craft business (Craft and Hobby Association www.craftandhobby.org) [there is a Web site dedicated to selling crafts at www.etsy.com], how to start a home-based photography business, and freelance food crafting—just to name a few.

Check the magazine section at your library. Observe what magazines the local branch patrons are subscribing to. This will give you some insight into what that neighborhood branch is interested in. In addition, it might be possible to check out magazines that are not a current issue.

Also, check out the Web site of your library. There are databases and other resources available to you just because you have a library card. For instance, some libraries subscribe to legal forms and provide free access to mailing list companies.

See if your library has **Mergent** Online. You can search industry and company profiles with the Business and Company Resource Center. Find demographic and market research data using the **ReferenceUSA** online resource.

In California (check your local state), if you have a California driver's license, you can get a library card from any California library and gain access to their library's Web site. In California and Nevada, a library card is provided free of charge to any resident of the state who wishes to borrow library materials or to use library resources. In Arizona, if you live within the city limits to use the library is free or $40 a year for a non-resident library card. We have recently seen California libraries charging a fee for non-county residents.

A resource that comes right to your mailbox are **community college catalogs**. These catalogs offer non-credit one-night seminars. Community services are looking for what interests' people. Watch for the classes that have just been added. If there was enough interest in the topic to add the class, it may be a hot topic!

Listen to people around you. What are they **whining** about? Go to fast food places and sit and listen to what people are talking about. Would that be something that you could create as a business?

There was a school teacher that listened to parents complaining, created a business of it and after a few years stopped teaching because the business was making more money. Each year, teachers have students with head lice. Parents hate the idea and treatment for the head lice. So a new business was developed. If you're interested, there is even a franchise for professional nitpickers!

People have been persuaded to become involved in a business that they knew nothing about, didn't understand, or didn't like. They saw others doing well and decided they could do it too. If you are not comfortable with—or do not believe in—the products or services, you are going to have a hard time getting enthusiastic about selling them. You are going to have an even harder time spending the time on the business after working hard all day (or resisting the temptation when your laundry calls your name).

If you try any of the resources in this book, please let us know how it went. Are they still in business? Do they offer what they say they do? We have done as much research as we could, but because we are not actually starting that type of business or service, our research doesn't go to the end. Help keep us up to date and pass your experiences along.

CHAPTER 2 Home-Based Businesses Using Computers

Start-up, home-based, mail order and Internet businesses can be an extension of existing skills you perform remotely from your home or a new set of skills you can learn or purchase software to achieve.

The businesses in this chapter assume that you have a computer system and Internet access. The actual computer system and access speed you will need depends on what you are planning to accomplish. You will need the ability to safely backup documents, setup and maintain password security, and read and write CD's and DVD's for delivery.

What computer equipment might you need to get started? Here is a general recommendation:

1. A 1.6 to 2.5 GHz desktop PC with Windows; 250 gigabyte hard drive, 2-3 gigabytes of RAM, keyboard, mouse, DVD R/W drive, multiple USB ports, audio and video I/O ports, and a good set of speakers.

2. A 17" LCD monitor with resolution of 1024 x 768 or higher.

3. A color ink jet printer capable of printing at least eight-pages per minute and a print resolution of 600 DPI or higher.

4. Microsoft Office Suite including Outlook, Word, PowerPoint, Excel, and Publisher.

5. Internet Explorer; Adobe Acrobat reader; Windows Media Player (these are FREE!).

6. High speed DSL or cable Internet access with the highest access speed you can afford.

7. External hard drive, USB 2.0 interconnect, 1 Terabyte of storage capability.

Note:

1. Macintosh equivalent hardware will work fine but be prepared to spend more for them.

2. A laptop computer will work for the basic configuration but is difficult and expensive to upgrade or expand compared to a desktop system.

3. Although other software packages, including FREE online programs are available, the Microsoft Office Suite programs are the preferred standard for business

Read **Making Money with Your Computer at Home** (1585424455) and also *Best Home Businesses for People 50+* (978-1585423804) by Paul and Sarah Edwards which is available at most libraries. We have personally used this book with a family member who is making money with his computer at home!

Several of the below services require formal credentialing, official certification of competency, and/or the ability and willingness to maintain confidentiality regarding both the information supplied and the results that the information and your efforts produce.

Although there are an endless number of possibilities for starting and running a computer business from your home, we have selected thirty-two of the most viable and lucrative, and have divided them into the following four categories:

• Ten businesses based on talent that you have.

• Eight businesses based on skills you can teach yourself.

• Six businesses based upon software and/or hardware you can purchase.

• Eight businesses based on skills that require formal training.

TALENT YOU HAVE

These opportunities assume that you already have the defined skills and are probably already offering them to an employer, as an employee, and would prefer to become an independent contractor and offer the same services from your home.

Book Cover Designer

> *"Anyone who believes that a book is NOT judged by its cover has never met a buyer from Barnes and Noble."*
> *Pam Shepard, a Barnes and Noble buyer*

To be successful, authors need to make sure their book gets looked at. Since the average bookstore browser spends eight seconds looking at the front cover and 15 seconds scanning the back cover, it's obvious that the cover is a critical part of the sales process.

Desktop publishing software compatible with the printing profession's systems is a mandate. This work may include the book cover itself and a dust jacket (for hardcover), and can also include logo design, sell sheets, promo items, business cards, postcards, bookmarks and almost anything else needed to ensure the book is a success.

Software required: desktop publishing and graphics software. Currently, this is specified as Quark Express, Indesign, or PageMaker. Other systems may be acceptable.

Business Plan Writer

A business plan is a document that summarizes the operational and financial objectives of a business and contains the detailed plans and budgets showing how the objectives are to be realized. Because the business plan contains detailed financial projections, forecasts about the business's performance, and a marketing plan, it is an incredibly useful tool for business planning. For anyone starting a business, it's a vital first step.

Software required: word processing, business plan, and spreadsheet. The bulk of the work is done with word processing software, and the financial elements involve spreadsheets. Preformatted business plan software packages assist in getting the entire plan properly packaged in an industry acceptable format.

Copywriter

A copyrighter is responsible for writing advertising copy and generating creative concepts, often in collaboration with an art director, creative director, someone who writes copy for advertisements, or someone who develops other promotional material. Most copywriters work in advertising or marketing, producing copy that is intended to persuade a customer to buy a product or service or otherwise take action.

Software required: word processing software. The work is done with word processing software, and occasionally with desktop publishing software, to format the final *look and feel* of the finished work as it will appear when printed.

Database Marketer

Everything from birth records, advertising lists, military service, and organization involvement are all in databases. 95 percent of the American public is listed and indexed in hundreds of separate databases. Databases contain demographic, geographic, and psychographic information about people that is used to perform target mailings (physical and virtual) to obtain more information or to sell something. The process of obtaining, maintaining, and utilizing these databases requires an intensive effort, especially, when list maintenance and hygiene is involved.

Software required: database management software and word processing with mail merge. The basic process requires you to have the same, or 100 percent compatible, database software as the client. If the client requires that the database be merged with other documents for mailing or data insertion, you will need the same word processing or mailing software they use.

Desktop Publisher

With more paper being generated than ever before, it is imperative that businesses produce high-quality printed documents that will get noticed and read. Desktop publishing allows you to take ideas and convert them directly into finished products that can be electronically, digitally, or conventionally reproduced.

Software required: desktop publishing and graphics software. The software enables you to see exactly how the document will appear when printed. If changes are needed, they can be implemented and viewed immediately. Once the document is complete, you can output it directly to a printer or you can produce a file and deliver it for production.

Employee Manual Writer

In today's litigious society, any company who hires employees must protect itself by creating, maintaining, and administering a written employee manual, to ensure that equity and fairness is maintained under all but the most extreme circumstances.

These manuals represent a contract between an employee and a company. It outlines the company's expectations of the employee, describes its responsibilities to the employee, and defines the benefits the employee will enjoy while working at the company. They include what the employee can expect from the company, the company's primary goals, employment classifications, policies, and standards.

Software required: word processing software. Word processing software and a good printer are usually all that are required. Once the manual is complete, it will likely be reviewed by the client's legal counsel. It may then be formatted and bound to be in concert with other official company documents.

Executive Search Consultant

Executive search consulting is a professional service provided to companies and organizations that need to locate and hire key employees. The service is paid for by the company or organization, not the job candidate. Potential candidates are identified, qualified, and presented to the client by the executive search firm based upon a job specification that is developed in conjunction with the client.

Assessing the candidate's degree of potential fit with the job specification is a key element for the search firm. This is important, since the most common reason a search consultant is engaged by a company or organization is to save the time and effort of identifying, qualifying, and reviewing potential candidates for specific leadership positions.

Software required: word processing, database, contact management, and Internet access. Since persistence and follow-up are *key* in these operations, contact management software such as Outlook, ACT! or Goldmine is an essential part of the process.

Financial Planner

Financial planning is the process of determining how an individual can meet his or her goals through the proper management of financial resources. Financial planners helps clients analyze all or selected areas of their finances. They develop a plan that brings together a client's financial goals, or provide advice on specific areas as needed. A plan does not necessarily have to be a written document; it can be financial recommendations or alternatives presented by the financial planner.

Software required: financial planning software. The software required depends on the planner's goals, objectives, and skills. It usually requires word processing software and some form of financial analysis software to present the dollar figures to the clients.

Freelancer

You may want to offer your services as a freelance copywriter. Check out the Web site **www.Elance.com**.

In addition to copywriting, Elance is also looking for: academic writing, accounting, accounts payable, accounts receivable, admin assistant, advertising, antitrust, Arabic translation, article writing, bankruptcy, benefits law, blogs, bookkeeping, branding, budgeting and forecasting, business analysis, business mathematics, business plans, business writing, children's writing, Chinese translation, commercial lending, compensation, computer, consumer protection, content writing, contract law, contracts, copyright, copywriting, corporate law, corporate strategy, creative and talent, creative writing, customer support, data entry, direct marketing, Dutch translation, e-books, editing, electronic commerce, e-mail handling, e-mail marketing, employment law, English, environment, event planner, family law, feature writing, fiction writing, financial analysis, financial forecasting, financial management, financial reporting, financial statements, financial writing, freelance marketing, French translation, general office skills, German translation, ghostwriting, Google AdSense, Google AdWords, Google analytics, Google Web master central, grammar, grant writing, helpdesk, immigration law, insurance, intellectual property, international law, Internet marketing, inventory management, investment research, and Italian translation.

Japanese translation, job costing, journalistic writing, Korean translation, Korean translation, Lacerte, lead generation, legal consulting, legal research, legal transcription, legal writing, legal writing, letter writing, letter writing, licensing, litigation, lyric writing, management, mandarin translation, market research, marketing strategy, medical billing, medical law, medical transcription, medical writing, Microsoft Office Outlook, Microsoft Office Word, negotiation, newsletters, non-fiction writing, office admin, online writing, organizational behavior, paralegal, patent law, payroll, Peachtree, poetry, Portuguese translation, press release, privacy, product liability, programming aptitude, project management, proofreading, proposal writing, public relations, public speaking, and punctuation.

QuickBooks, Quicken, real estate law, records management, report writing, research, résumé writing, Russian translation, sales letters, sales writing, sales, screenwriting, script writing, Spanish translation, Spanish, speech writing, spelling, sports writing, statistics, strategic planning, Swedish translation, tax law, tax preparation, technical writing, telemarketing, telephone etiquette, telephone handling, time management, trade law, trademark, transcription, travel planning, travel writing, trusts estates wills, typing, Ukrainian translation, user guides, Web content, word processing, word, and WordPerfect.

Elance deducts from 6.75 percent and 8.75 percent for your payment for this service.

www.99Designs.com is similar to Elance, however, the price/fee is listed first. The categories they have are: logos, business cards, stationery, brochures, newsletters, Web banners, and Web billboards.

You might also like to check out http://beaguide.about.com. They have experts (guides) that write on a specific subject only. Some of the topics that were available were: 4-wheel driving, black hair, bowling, corvettes, and rodeo. Also http://becomeaguide.chacha.com has something similar.

Résumé Writer

Employers are busy. When reviewing an applicant's résumé, most reviewers look for certain key words or specific experiences that indicate a fit between the applicant and the position. Résumé writing has become an art form, with the résumé writer acting in the role of a topic specialist who emphasizes a person's specific strengths for the job under consideration.

Realistically, a good résumé writer can fine-tune applicants' résumés so that they do not ramble on about insignificant details that, while truthful, are of no interest to the prospective employer.

Software required: word processing software and résumé templates.

Technical Writer

Technical writing usually involves analyzing information and creating reports and instruction sets, then making recommendations based on the material and information supplied.

Software required: word processing software and specialty software. This usually requires nothing more than word processing software, although specific disciplines may require the use of certain fonts, formats, or templates specific to a particular industry or compliance standard.

YOUR HOBBY

What do you like to do? Do you love computers? How about plastics? Are you interested in metals? Or in manufacturing? Can you sit and talk about antiques endlessly with your friends? Does your conversation always turn to airplanes? Or to food? Do you have an industry with which you are familiar? Have you been on the distribution end of a particular field? Are you in retail? Do you enjoy catalogs?

What are you good at? Are you a good writer? A great chef? Do you enjoy working with your hands? Are you creative? Are you good at design? Are you good at art? Are you skillful at creating mechanical objects? Are you a great negotiator? Are you detail oriented? Do you have a special gift in any one area?

Look at your hobbies. You know what products sell, because you are buying them. You know where to find customers because you are a customer. You know what a good bargain is because you have looked all over. You have a depth of knowledge to draw on—use it! That's what one of the authors, Nancy, did. Her hobby is the British Royal family and she sold royal collectibles. Listen to what people are asking about or for because that could be your business.

All of these passions are great pursuits in which you can get involved. Read! Visit the library, bookstore, or newsstand. Examine the classified section of the numerous magazines, weeklies, and newspapers for products. Surf the Internet's online bookstores titles for ideas.

Your Exercise

Here is an exercise to help you discover what you are good at. Write down a list of your talents, what you like to do, or what you're good at. After the first couple of minutes, keep thinking and add to the list. After you're done, go back to the list and cross off the top three or four items.

There is something about us humans: the top items on our list are the things that we are trying to do, something we want to do or something somebody told us we should do. Those items listed in the middle are going to be those things that you do naturally. Because they come easy to us, we typically discount our talent saying, "Everyone can do that."

For many years, Nancy was giving presentations on the British Royal family. Her partner, Mike, suggested that she write a book and start teaching seminars on how to get organized. Nancy's response was, "There are already so many people doing that and it's so easy to do, everyone can do it."

Finally heeding his advice, Nancy wrote *Clutterology® Getting Rid of Clutter and Getting Organized,* which is now in its fourth edition, and she has spoken before thousands of students. Helping people to get organized was truly one of Nancy's natural talents.

SKILLS YOU CAN TEACH YOURSELF

Many of the software programs available for today's computers are of the *do-it-yourself* variety. They require only that you teach yourself how to use them and then that you have the time and patience to apply what you have learned.

The logic behind offering the service stems from the time and frustration involved with both the learning curve and the complex operational aspects, and from the fact that many people would prefer to pay someone else to do this for them.

Data Conversion Technician

Y2K brought the awareness that many database systems had serious inequities and needed to be converted to more modern formats. What's more important, is that it brought to light the fact that database maintenance is both important to an organization and one of the most time consuming and tedious processes to maintain.

Everything from Web generated e-mail lists to complex profile analysis of database information is being outsourced.

The software requirements will usually be dictated by the client even though the skills are pretty much universal across all platforms. They include the ability to type rapidly and accurately, the patience to check all entries for completeness, correct spelling and required information.

You will have to allow a percentage of time for data correction since errors and changes occur constantly. You will also need to learn how to import and export to and from different database programs as required by the client's needs.

Software required: database management software (type dependant).

Digital Album Organizer

With good digital cameras priced at under $100, people are shooting hundreds of photos and transferring them to their hard drive for titling, sorting, and storage as an electronic photo album. The problem is that most people never get around to doing anything except storing them on a hard drive or CD-ROM.

Although there are many outstanding album software programs available, most people don't have the time or patience to organize their digital photos, and they would be glad to pay to have their material put into a format they would use and could leave as a legacy.

Software required: digital album software. This takes organizational skills. You may need an audio recorder to interview the photo owner about the date, people involved, titling, and descriptions for each of the photos so you can add them to the album listing.

Digital Image Operator

Whether digital or film, most photos rarely look as good as they could. Historically, improving photos was an expensive and complicated process. With digital imagery, everything is a possibility, from red-eye elimination and changing backgrounds to editing in and editing out backgrounds and people.

This discipline requires patience. The software is forgiving and mistakes are rarely permanent or fatal—you reedit the changes and continue on. The market for this service varies from professional photography for advertising and promotional campaigns to family portrait shots.

Software required: graphic and photograph editing software.

Form Designer

Organizations are streamlining as much of their data as possible by using standardized forms. The logic is that the standardization of data forces uniformity while providing a streamlined environment for the searching and categorizing of data.

Many of the forms are being put on the Internet for uniformity and ease of data input, and need to be user-friendly. Some of the forms need to perform calculations or provide preformatted data, such as credit card selection or specifically limited choices (color or size).

Effective forms exhibit two characteristics: simplicity and uniformity. Unfortunately, obtaining these characteristics is time consuming and tedious—making it a perfect task for outsourcing. There are two software approaches to creating forms: use forms software specifically designed for the purpose and create forms from scratch.

High-end forms software and Acrobat have several options, including printing. More important is the ability to lock certain parts of the document (like the legends for the fields) and unlock others (like the information to be filled in by the customers). Once the forms are filled in and downloaded, the data can be imported into one or more databases for storage, retrieval, and manipulation.

Software required: word processing software, form design software and Adobe Acrobat. Acrobat is a powerful conversion program that essentially creates a snapshot of the document you created. Once created, the document is converted to the PDF (Portable Document Format), which is essentially unchangeable by the customer and is universally readable on Windows, Macintosh, and other formats without any distortion or errors.

PowerPoint Presentations Designer

PowerPoint is currently the world's most popular electronic slide show software. The latest versions provide a variety of animation, sounds, and other special effects that provide a presenter with dynamic eye-catching presentations to keep the audience interested and involved.

These dynamic presentations come with a cost—a lot of time and effort. Plus, the best slides require an eye for graphics, color, and graphics balance. Creating good PowerPoint slides is a graphics art function.

Software required: PowerPoint and graphics software. The recommendation is to have the latest version of PowerPoint along with a graphics program to generate and manipulate the artwork you will be adding to the slides. The latest version will save the final work in several of the older versions so you will be assured of compatibility with the client's system.

Several firms offer a range of optional backgrounds, sound effects, and a wide range of graphics and fonts to enhance the overall power of the package. (Check out the new software program called Ovation www.Adobe.com.)

A valuable accessory called Producer is available as a free download from www.Microsoft.com. This program allows you to convert manually advanced PowerPoint presentations into an automated, user controllable presentation, complete with background music, video, and narration.

Video Editor

Video cameras abound, and just about every new computer comes with video editing software—albeit simplistic. The problem for the weekend videographers is that it still takes time and effort to convert the raw video from a season's worth of little league baseball or an entire Christmas pageant into something you want to look at and keep.

As a video editor, you will take the raw material, arrange it in a logical sequence, title it, narrate it, add background music and special effects, and return the edited material to the owners in a finalized form. You might even provide copies for a fee.

Software required: video editing software and hardware. Excellent software packages start at under $100 and additional effects and music are available as upgrades. Here are the key points: it takes about 14 gigabytes of hard drive for each hour of raw video you import for editing, and the import drive has to be a high speed type to accommodate the video transfer rate. Other considerations are the speed of the computer, amount of memory, video input ports, and the ability to create final material.

Virtual Consumer Service Agent

Would you like to stay home and sit on the phone for a couple hours a day answering people's questions, making airline reservations or flower orders? If so here are two organizations to contact: www.LiveOps.com, www.AlpineAccess.com and www.Arise.com.

These organizations have strict standards. They may require that you have graduated from high school or have a GED. Also, while you are on the phone, the environment must be quiet. No barking dogs, crying children or other sounds that will carry through the telephone lines.

These companies will also charge a fee. LiveOps (about $50) and AlpineAccess (about $45) for a personal credit check. Out-of-pocket and preliminary cost for Arise for the background check, personal credit check, purchase of required equipment and incorporation costs could be as high as $600.

Work at home customer support opportunities (billing inquiry, purchase an accessory, or product assistance/troubleshooting) are available at www.West.com.

While www.TeleReach.com is a telemarketing company looking for people who already have business to business, cold calling, tele-prospecting, outside sales or appointment setting experience. www.ConvergysWorkAtHome.com is looking for customer service and billing service help.

www.Intrep.com is looking for people who have the ability to set appointments with prospects, an extensive sales and marketing background, a complete understanding of business-related software and are high achievers and self-motivated. You must pass their personality and proficiency tests. You set your own hours and generally do not travel.

Working Solutions (www.WorkingSol.com) utilizes highly educated and trained professionals who have great communication and multilingual skills. Agents have knowledge of specific products and industries to meet specific business needs. www.ACDDirect.com is resource for a career as a call center agent.

If you are a mother who is looking for part-time work, check out M.U.M.S. (Mothers Utilizing Many Skills) which is a division of The Daisy Chain. Call them at 310-316-3633. There is also a Web site call www.HireMyMom.com which is similar to M.U.M.S. and also Work At Home Moms (www.WAHM.com).

www.Tutor.com works with high-level math (algebra 2, geometry, and trigonometry), science (chemistry, physics), social studies, and English tutors a minimum of five hours a week between Sunday and Thursday from 4 PM to 11 PM during the academic year. Need additional sources, go to your local library's Web site. They probably provide a tutoring program. Find the name of the tutoring program and contact them directly.

Tutoring as a Successful Business (978-0967236100) by Eileen Kaplan Shapiro, The National Tutoring Association (www.ntatutor.org) has training and certification. On another hand, if you're interested in purchasing a franchise, check out www.Abrakadoodle.com.

If you are a nurse, Google (or use your favorite search engine) "phone triage nurse" and there are several Web sites listed.

Web Site Designer

The Internet is a lot of computers that can talk to each other, and the Web is a gigantic library of stored information that exists within this enormous network of computers. Effective Web site design is the ability to take raw data and other pertinent information and format it into a user-friendly style for storage on a Web site. Once it has been electronically published on the site, it becomes accessible to anyone who has access to the Web.

The best Web site designers are NOT necessarily the best graphic artists (although having graphic arts capabilities can be an asset). They are usually the ones who understand what the creator of the site is trying to accomplish and what the customer wants or needs to get from the site to be satisfied that it has fulfilled its purpose.

Software required: Web site design software. Software packages from the freebies that come with Web site hosting through the most sophisticated programs all provide the ability to start with standard templates and pretty them up as needed. The most important thing for a site to be considered successful is to create the site with the customers in mind. After all, the customers are the ones who come looking for the information.

SOFTWARE AND/OR HARDWARE YOU CAN PURCHASE

Here are some recommendations for hardware and software you can purchase to get your business up and running in the shortest amount of time.

If you have taken a class at the community college, keep the receipts as you may be eligible for the student discount when you purchase software.

Audiotape and Records to CD Conversion Technician

First there were records and then came cassette tapes. Now, there are CD's, and most people want to listen to their old records and tapes on their new CD players.

Software required: conversion software, audio cassette deck, CD recorder, and a turntable for records. The hardware and software needed to perform these conversion functions are relatively inexpensive. The process is time consuming, especially if you are going to reduce or eliminate the clicks, pops, hisses, and other noises that have contaminated the original medium.

You will want a good label making software program so that you can give your client a spiffy looking, four-color label instead of a plain black and white label listing on the CD's face. CD/DVD Label Making Software $21.95 www.Acoustica.com 952-908-4090.

An alternative to this would be CD to iPod conversion. If you used iTunes at $0.99 a song to fill the latest iPod, it would cost nearly $30,000.00.

Videotape to DVD Conversion Technician

Videotapes are officially defunct as of January 2009 and have been replaced with DVD's. The reasons include both quality of the DVD's and the deterioration factor of the videotape material itself. The result is that many consumers are concerned that their videotapes are going to be unplayable in a few years and what them converted.

Software required: videotape player, conversion hardware, conversion software, and DVD recorder. There are a variety of hardware conversion tools you can use in conjunction with your computer. These are current model numbers, so check for the latest version. You can also shop for deals!

Additional Software Suggestions:

- Adobe Acrobat $300-$500 www.Adobe.com 800-585-0774

- Adobe Elements $140 www.Adobe.com 800-585-0774

- Computers and backup hard drives $500-$5,000 Tiger Direct www.TigerDirect.com 800-800-8300 or CompUSA stores

- FormTool 5 Form design software $50-$150 www.FormTool.com 888-459-0078

- Microphones and mixers $500-$1000 Guitar Center www.GuitarCenter.com 866-498-7882

- Microsoft Expression Web $100 www.Microsoft.com 800-642-7676 or Adobe Dreamweaver $200 www.Adobe.com 800-585-0774

- Microsoft Producer free www.Microsoft.com 800-642-7676

- Paint Shop Pro Software $80 www.Microsoft 800-642-7676

- Pinnacle Studio video editing software with multi-input box $149 www.PinnacleSys.com 866-446-0833

- PowerPoint 2010 $100 www.Microsoft.com 800-642-7676

- CD/DVD Duplicators $200-$1600 Shop4Tech www.Shop4Tech.com 866-907-3626.

- Turntable, software and tape deck $350 www.DAK.com.

- Videotape to DVD converters Sony DVDirect VRDVC20 DVD+/-RW DL Standalone DVD Recorder 250 TigerDirect www.TigerDirect.com 800-800-8300 or CompUSA stores

Backup Service Provider

Not fully backing up your computer files is an invitation to disaster. Although we all know we should backup our computers on a regular basis, few people do it often enough and many people, including businesses, don't do it at all. The importance of this becomes apparent when (not if) a hard drive disaster occurs and the business suddenly discover that the one and only copy of their most important data files just went up in a magnetic storm.

The Internet, high-speed access, allows remote backup services to be offered to individuals and businesses. The service can be offered as needed or, preferably, as a subscription service where the data is backed up and stored on a regularly scheduled basis. The storage medium can be CD, DVD, or hard drive. We recommend DVD due to the storage capability versus cost factor and fees for secure storage of the backup data. This cost can be included in the service.

Software required: computer with dual drives, copying software, Internet access, file sharing software, hard drive backup system, and a DVD recorder.

CD/DVD Copying Service Technician

If there was ever a business that lent itself to being run from home, it is the copying of CDs and DVDs. Amateur sports events, garage bands, school plays, professional event advertising and product demonstrations all need to be duplicated. The business of duplicating, labeling, and packaging disks has become a volume business. Most people who need more than one or two copies of their material prefer to pay to have the service accomplished.

The low overhead of a home-based business is an advantage; the actual process requires about a kitchen table's worth of space and a minimum investment to get started. The actual process of copying/duplicating is simple. Because it's time consuming, it requires the proper equipment and a little training.

Systems for making duplications abound. These include simple techniques as a CD/DVD read/write drive with Nero (www.Nero.com) burning software in a personal computer on through and including multiple disk copying systems that provide a high-speed duplication of virtually any disk format.

In addition to duplicating the discs, the services can include copying and applying all paper labels to the disks or, as an alternative, screen printing the graphics and text information right on the disk itself. You can consider supplying the packaging for the disks. This includes the cases, printed inserts, and the insertion of the disk into the case. If you are interested, you can acquire a shrink-wrap machine and shrink-wrap the finished packages.

The resources listed below can provide you with all the equipment you will need to accomplish this function.

Blank media, labels, and cases www.Shop4Tech.com 866-907-3626

Disk duplication systems www.ProActionMedia.com 877-593-4261

Nero duplication software for personal computers www.SoftwareOutlet.com 714-979-6161

Digital Recording Studio Engineer

Most recordings have gone completely digital because of its perfect fidelity, ease of capture and editing, and the fact that it's about the cheapest recording media ever invented.

Software required: audio inputs (microphones, mixers, etc), editing software, and mixing software, and CD recorder. Most computer systems, from an old 486 on up, will work as a beautiful digital recorder as long as you invest a few bucks in a good sound card, editing software, and a big hard drive.

Multimedia Technician

Reduced costs of high-speed computers, memory, and high capacity hard drives, have made professional quality video and audio editing affordable for the home-based professional. You will need a dedicated computer system and the ability to import a variety of tape formats. To output the data, you will need software and hardware to supply the client with formats as specified.

Software required: video and audio input sources, video editing software, multimedia software, CD and DVD recorders.

The editing software you use will be dictated by the client's requirements. Most of the name brand programs will provide the versatility and flexibility for all but the most sophisticated applications.

SKILLS THAT REQUIRE FORMAL TRAINING

If you have a skill or trade that does not require that you be at the same physical location as the person requesting the work, you are a candidate for taking the service off-site and offering it as an independent contractor from your home.

There is an online company where you can take online classes. Some of the classes offer a certificate upon completion. It is **www.Ed2Go.com**. Many colleges offer classes through this company. If you go directly to the Web site, you may have a greater number of courses to choose from. The only difference if you go through the college (www.Ed2Go.com/GCC [Glendale Community College] for instance) is that the fee is split 1/3 to the Web site, 1/3 to the instructor and 1/3 to the school. The majority of the courses are only $89.

Association Management Provider

With the diversity of professions and personal interests, associations that bring together people who have a common interest are growing at a phenomenal rate. The National Trade and Professional Associations (NTPA) directory lists over 10,000 associations in the United States, and the number is increasing each year. When you include the local and regional chapters for these groups, the number of organizations requiring managements soars past 100,000.

When they are small and new, associations are staffed and administered by the individuals actively involved with the association. As the size of the group increases, so do the logistics and time required to keep the association alive, well, and in compliance with its current rules, regulations, bylaws, and mandates.

Membership, recordkeeping, financial matters, and other business related matters are often subcontracted to firms that specialize in association management. The basic requirements are knowledge of the basic business requirements for the association and the software required to support business logistics.

Software required: word processing software with mail merge capability, accounting software, and database management software.

Additional software required may include spreadsheets, desktop publishing and Web site software depending on your skill level and the organization's requirements.

Billing and Invoicing Provider

Many small and medium businesses are good at what they do, but they lack the time and skills to keep their accounting and billing accurate and up to date. Obviously, in order to survive, businesses need to keep their cash flow current and positive. When the accounting and invoicing becomes a nuisance to their daily business activities, they contract for outside services.

Software required: word processing software with mail merge capability, accounting software, and database management software.

The primary software requirements include word processing software for writing letters and other related correspondence plus accounting software that fits the structure of the client's business. In some cases, clients will insist that the software you use be exactly the same as they currently use, or as their financial and tax account has specified.

We have known individuals who specialize in providing this type of service to veterinarians and chiropractors.

Bookkeeping Provider

Lots of businesses and individuals use the shoebox technique for keeping their records and then, when they have problems with the IRS, regret not keeping accurate records. The ability to derive financial order from the chaos of someone else's disorganization is a marketable skill.

Just because you can balance your own checkbook doesn't mean that you have the credentials of a bookkeeper. To offer your services as a bookkeeper, you must have a certificate.

If you elect to provide this service, be prepared to initially spend a lot of time getting the client to explain the mountains of scrap paper, incomplete receipts, and missing paperwork that almost inevitably accompany this need. You will need to establish written guidelines for clients to follow so that you are not constantly straightening out their financial messes.

Software required: word processing software with mail merge capability, accounting software, and database management software.

Medical Transcription Provider

With each passing day, new rules, regulations, and guideline are demanding that medical personnel completely and accurately document their procedures, prescriptions, consultations, and patient appointments in a timely manner. Busy medical personnel seldom have enough time to type and edit their own reports, so the process of dictating and recording, coupled with transcription services, has long been an established method of keeping patient files up to date.

To offer this service, you will have to invest in a dedicated phone line or two, plus some form of automated voice-messaging program for your computer. This will allow a physician to call in and record while simultaneously giving you the ability to playback and transcribe the material.

The person doing the transcription can be anywhere so long as he or she has telephone access. That way doctors can call and record their notes on the transcriber's computer, and then the transcriber can return the finished documents via the Internet.

Software required: word processing software, laser printer, Internet access, recording and playback equipment.

The software required is normally no more than word processing software. You will need knowledge of the medical terminology used plus an electronic spellchecker for medical terms.

Medical Claims Specialist

As the medical profession becomes more dependent on the insurance industry, it relies more and more on the ability of a claims assistant to cross-reference patient's tests, diagnoses, and treatment with an allowable insurance claim number, since this is becoming the primary basis for payment and reimbursement for drugs and services.

As with many other jobs, this one is not dependant on the person being in the same physical locale as the physician performing the services. In fact, in the final analysis, it makes no difference whether the claims assistant is in the same office or across the world—the service is performed independently of the physician and the results can be mailed, faxed, or e-mailed to the individual or department that needs them to complete the billing cycle.

Software required: word processing software with mail merge capability and database management software.

Secretarial Services Provider

Even though computers surround us, and everybody seems to have two or more of them, many people still prefer to handwrite their notes, letters, drafts, and manuscripts. Speech recognition notwithstanding, a lot of people prefer to dictate their notes, thoughts, and opinions. These people need someone to convert their writing into computer generated word processing files. When grammar, form, style, and spelling are involved, the service required is commonly called editing. When the entire work needs to be written, the need is for a ghostwriter. The answer to all of these dilemmas is to hire someone to wordsmith the material and turn it into presentable, grammatically correct documentation.

The process requires knowledge of typing, grammar, and business letter formatting. If the work is done in a specific discipline—such as engineering or medicine—a working knowledge of the terminology, technology, and buzzwords currently being used is also a requirement.

Software required: word processing software and a laser printer.

Check out **www.IVAA.org** which is the Web site for the International Virtual Assistant Association. Join as a member ($125 dues). They provide conferences and also provide a referral service.

In addition to providing certification as a VA, people can submit a RFP (request for proposal), contact information and description of the needs. IVAA members reply directly back to the inquiry.

Some of the service categories are: accounting and bookkeeping; association management; coaching support; concierge services; database design and management; desktop publishing; editing and proofreading; executive assistance; graphic design and editing; Internet commerce; language translation; legal and paralegal services; live phone answering; mailing services; marketing and advertising; multimedia presentations; nonprofit support; other administrative services; project management; real estate support; research and development; transcription services; Web site design; word processing and typing.

Tax Preparer

Tax preparation services have been fully computerized since the mid 1980's. Advances in computer software—especially full access via the Internet to tax sites, the IRS, and the ability to transfer the client's tax forms as attachments has given accountants the ability to operate remotely. The critical component is for the client to have 100 percent compatible software to the tax preparer's. That way when the client creates records for use in the tax filings, which they don't have to be reentered.

Software required: tax preparation software and a laser printer.

Translator

The world has gone global and every form of goods and services imaginable is being imported, exported, and utilized by the most diverse cultural group in history. Effectively providing all of these requires all sorts of documents to be translated into the customers' native languages. If you speak, read, and write multiple languages, all you need is a word processor and the appropriate keyboard conversion software to allow you to format, display, and print things like Cyrillic characters.

Software required: word processing software with appropriate language packages, laser printer, CD recorder, and Internet access.

See also the information about IVAA and Elance.

CHAPTER 3 Products and Services to Offer

There are many storefront businesses that can be successfully operated as a home-based business. If you want to find what's currently hot, Google (or use your favorite search engine) the *top 10 small business ideas* and you will find many more ideas. However, what's hot today may not be hot tomorrow. Use the information of what's hot to find your passion. Always go with what you know.

HOME-BASED BUSINESS

Here are 70 suggestions of the type of home-based businesses prominent at this time. If you find one that appeals to you, research it further. Use this list to start brainstorming your own ideas. These are in alphabetical order.

1. Apartment management
2. Association management services
3. Astrology charting services
4. Backup service
5. Ballroom decorating
6. Basic video editing
7. Beads
8. Billing and invoicing service
9. Book cover design
10. Bookkeeping service
11. Business of sewing
12. Business plan writer
13. Candles
14. Cartooning
15. Certified tax preparer
16. Child visitation monitor
17. Children after school
18. Citrus growing
19. Clown
20. Coaching (life)
21. Concierge services (www.ICLMA.org) (www.ConciergeAssoc.org)
22. Copywriter
23. Culinary services
24. Data conversion services
25. Database marketing services
26. Decorate homes to sell
27. Desktop publishing
28. Digital album organization
29. Digital image manipulation
30. Digital recording studio services
31. eBay
32. Employee manual writing
33. Event planner
34. Executive search
35. Financial planning
36. Floral or florist
37. Form design service
38. Get paid to travel
39. Handyman service

40. Import and export
41. Interior decorator
42. Landscape
43. Legal transcription services
44. Loan signing agent
45. Magazine writing
46. Medical insurance billing
47. Mosaic table tops and steps
48. Multimedia production
49. Mystery shopper#
50. Non-medical in home care
51. Notary services
52. Photography
53. Picture frame
54. PowerPoint presentations
55. Quilting
56. Real estate appraisal
57. Record to CD conversion
58. Résumé writer
59. Secretarial services
60. Soap making
61. Substitute teacher
62. Tapestry
63. Technical writing
64. Tele-worker
65. Videotape to DVD conversion
66. Web site design
67. Wired jewelry
68. Woodworking
69. Word processing
70. Yoga

Resources for mystery shopper classes:

Elaine Moran 909-463-6359 is the instructor for many of these classes and has a book available or can be reached at mstgroup@verizon.net.

Cerritos College www.CerritosCommunityEd.com 562-467-5050 x 2521.

Mount San Jacinto College www.MSJC.edu 951-487-6752 x 3711 course number #9208.

Saddleback College www.Saddleback-CE.com 949-582-4646 course number #675.

MAIL ORDER BUSINESSES

A mail order business is any business where the product is shipped (mailed) to the customer. This includes catalogs, mail order businesses, Internet businesses and eBay businesses.

Catalogs

The good news about catalogs is that they are popular and have been around for a long time and they will continue to be around for a long time in the future.

It's estimated that consumers and businesses combined spend roughly $150 billion on catalog purchases per year. Since catalogs are risky and expensive, listen to the customer—are they asking to have a catalog sent to them? Run a test ad—first see if it will pay off. Get help from trade experts.

Consumers who receive catalogs are more likely to become frequent buyers online, accounting for 15 percent more transactions, and will spend on average 16 percent more than customers who did not receive catalogs. Consumers who receive catalogs in the mail are more than twice as likely to make an online purchase according to a post by Alex on August 10, 2011 by Alex for *Advantages of Catalog Marketing*.

A survey found the hot categories of products in catalog sales rank sales were:

1. Apparel   3. Books, music and videos   5. Electronics

2. Gifts   4. Home furnishings

Catalog printing is a specialty. Contact your local printer and ask for a referral of a catalog printer. The catalog printer provides some assistance with their services. It can take four to five months to produce a full-color catalog. Building a catalog business takes time, so don't hold your breath. Catalog Age is a trade magazine for catalog pros.

Mail Order

What products and services are runaway bestsellers right now for mail order? The answers may surprise you. Here is a list of a top ten mail order catalogs by category according to the company *Change Of Address*.

1. Clothing   6. Gifts and Collectibles

2. Computers and Electronics   7. Baby and Toys for Children

3. Cars, Trucks, Cycles   8. Home Décor

4. Books, Music, and Movies   9. Sports and Recreation

5. Office Supplies   10. Hobbies, and Crafts

Internet

Online sales of consumer according to Forrester Research and Barclays Capital's *Internet Data Book* in 2009. The first group is online sales by category (in no specific order) and the second column is online buying preference of a product (in no specific order):

1. Pet products   5. Apparel

2. Food and beverage   6. Auto parts

3. Over-the-counter medicines   7. Consumer electronics

4. Personal care items

1. Books and magazines

2. Clothing

3. Electronics

4. Food, Beer and Wine

5. Furniture

6. Music and Video

7. Office Supplies

8. Toys and games

Bidding For Good Auction

There are other auction sites that are popping up. We're familiar with www.cmarket.com/auction/BiddingForGood.action which is an auction site for charities. You may want to drop into this site and check out how they do things and what you would change.

This site has become a valuable resource for us. Here are some of the ways that we us it:

- With the current condition of the economy, you may be seeing a lot of empty advertising spaces including billboard and bus benches. Although the prices may be down, check out BiddingForGood and search the auctions to find if there are good deals for discounted advertising. We have found billboards, bus benches, a full page in USA Today (regional edition), and full-page ads in an association publication.

- Search for words like billboard, advertising, full-page and full page. You may get the front cover, back cover, or some good deals for a fraction of the cost.

- If you are looking to attract customers, perhaps donating your product or service to an auction (or several) may draw the clients you're looking for.

- Look at the ad copy of the items. Would you be willing to spend your money on that item? If not, why not. Look over the site to get some good ideas what you would do on your Web site and what you won't do on your Web site. Are the key questions answered about what the product is?

- We have purchased several items that have been on our Bucket List (a life-long dream list). Nancy recently purchased a submarine ride for Mike.

eBay

If you were shopping on eBay, the top most wanted products would be:

1. Nintendo DS

2. Coupons

3. BMW

4. iPod

5. Blackberry Torch

6. Shoes

7. Blackberry

8. Kindle

9. iPhone

10. MacBook

You may notice that at this time, most of the hot products on eBay are electronic and the newest version. To find out what is hot on eBay, in the upper left corner, under SELL, click on What's Hot.

FRANCHISE, BUSINESS OPPORTUNITY AND TV INFOMERCIALS

Although they sound like they are the same thing, franchises, business opportunities and television infomercials are very different.

Franchise

A franchise is a proven method of doing business that has a proven success formula. There have been a variety of successful franchises for home-based businesses. Some involve using a pre-developed catalog such as stationery supplies or gift items.

The franchisor, by its very definition and legal requirements, requires that the franchisee strictly adhere to the policies, procedures, and guidelines of the franchise manual. The logic is that the process has been proven by trial and error; to deviate from the proven method will result in failure. In other words, a franchise is a proven success formula and your purchase of the franchise requires that you adhere to it.

One of the best resources we have come across lately for helping you decide whether or not to buy a franchise or not is David Bach's book **Start Late, Finish Rich** (0767919467). In chapter 18, he covers buying a franchise. According to Bach:

Top Ten Low-Cost Franchises:

1. Curves
2. 7-Eleven Inc.
3. Jackson Hewitt Tax Service
4. Jani-King
5. Kuman Math and Reading Center
6. Chem-Dry
7. Service Master Clean
8. REMAX International
9. Jan-Pro International
10. Merle Norman

Top Ten Home-Based Franchises:

1. Jani-King
2. Chem-Dry
3. Service Master Clean
4. Snap-on Tools
5. Jan-Pro Franchising
6. Jazzercise Inc.
7. Matco Tools
8. Servpro
9. CleanNet USA Inc.
10. Coverall Cleaning Concepts

Ninety-five percent of franchises are in operation after five years while national statistics for business are 95 percent of businesses are not in operation after five years.

Robert T. Kiyosaki is the author of *Rich Dad, Poor Dad*. He operates on the 95 percent failure ratio. His first several businesses failed. Then he was successful with the *Rich Dad, Poor Dad* business. When he started his next business, he went back to the 95 percent statistic. Just because he was successful once, didn't mean that he would be successful again.

Check out www.Entrepreneur.com; www.Franchise.org; www.FranData.com; and the American Association of Franchisees and Dealers (AAFFD) www.AAFD.org for additional information.

Business Opportunity

A business opportunity is another concept entirely. A business opportunity is a *buy-the-manual-and-develop-it-yourself-and-hope-you-get-lucky* method.

It is a set of business ideas and guidelines that may or may not have proven successful. There are no legal requirements on a business opportunity other than the truth-in-advertising laws that say that whatever the seller promises, the seller must deliver. Many business opportunities exist for the home-based business that work, that do not work, that work sometimes, and that work for some people but not for others.

Because business opportunities involve a variety of skills, budgets, facilities, and experience, they should be investigated carefully to ensure that they are appropriate for your needs, objectives, goals, and capabilities. (Believe it or not, you can find business opportunities on eBay.) A magazine that sells businesses and products is Small Business Opportunity Magazine (www.SBOMag.com).

If you want to check out a business opportunity before spending money, check out www.FTC.gov or 877-382-4357. The typical complaint is cheap or low-quality of merchandise, poor quality equipment, or poor location. Get a copy of their earnings statement in writing before you make a commitment.

On the state level, contact the attorney general and inquire if there has been anything filed on the company that you are thinking about investing in.

Call the city hall in which the business is located. Ask for a reliability report. Also call the chamber of commerce and ask if there is any reason why not to do business with the company you are investigating.

What is better for you, a franchise or a business opportunity (starting your own business)? Have you ever been fired from a job? If so, you may be better suited to a business opportunity. When you buy a franchise, you need to do things the franchisor's way. If you have great ideas or want to go in a different direction, the franchisor usually does not allow that.

TV Infomercials

Late night infomercials have been part of our life for many years. The offers seem incredible and fantastic. So should we invest our hard earned money in these offers? That is entirely up to you. What we can say is that the information on these commercials has to be documented. Does that mean that your results will be the same? Not necessarily, it just means that one person, one time had that result.

If you are interested in a product or service offered on television, use the Internet to do some research. For instance, use Google (or use your favorite search engine) and do a search for the name of the product and the word scam.

Another suggestion that one of our students made was to Google the name of the person who's giving the testimonial of the product. If you Google the company name, nothing negative may come up. However, by checking for the name of the person giving the testimonial you may find that person may have a negative business history. It's easy to change the name of the business. It's harder to have great testimonials.

Multilevel

Multilevel marketing (MLM) (also called network marketing) is a business model that combines direct marketing with franchising. In a typical multilevel marketing or network marketing arrangement, individuals associate with a parent company as an independent contractor and are compensated based on their sales of products or service, as well as the sales achieved by those they bring into the business.

In a legitimate MLM company, commissions are earned only on sales of the company's products. No money may be earned from recruiting alone (sign-up fees). MLM businesses do operate legitimately in all 50 United States and more than 100 other countries, and new businesses may use terms like affiliate marketing or home-based business franchising.

Examples frequently include multilevel businesses such as Amway, Shaklee, Nu Skin, Mary Kay, and Tupperware. Now, there are more multilevel or network marketing companies out there than ever.

A colleague of ours gives seminars about multilevel marketing. Eric Alexander is an MLM corporate professional who has created programs, trained personnel, and written manuals. He knows from first-hand experience that the primary problem is that most people who join an MLM organization do NOT get the proper training required to make it a success. His seminars shows people the real insights and techniques, as proven by the major MLM companies, required for individuals to make a minimal investment and be successful. Eric may be reached at 800-961-9461 or magiceric@cox.net.

SCAMS

Sometimes when an offer seems too good, too easy or promises too much money they probably aren't what they say they are. One of the first indications of a scam is the request for money before you really know what they are offering or what you'll be getting. Here are a couple of typical scams to watch out for.

Work-At-Home Offers

Beware! Work-at-home schemes do not guarantee regular salaried employment. They will require you to invest your money before you learn how a plan works or before you are sent instructions. The work you are asked to do often continues the fraud by getting other victims involved.

The most common type of work-at-home fraud is envelope stuffing. Typically, there are no envelopes to stuff. Instead, you receive instructions on how to deceive others by placing an ad like the one to which you responded! Other schemes require you to assemble gift and specialty products for which there is little or no market.

Our research has found E F Lindbloom Co, 3636 W Peterson Ave, Chicago IL 60659-3274 claiming that they are the only company that shows you a genuine way to make money addressing and mailing envelopes. If you are interested in stuffing envelopes, check them out with caution.

Suspect any ad claiming you can earn an unusually high income with little or no effort on your part.

Government Grant Money

You may have received an e-mail stating something about claiming your share of Government Grant Money to pay your mortgage, start a business or expand your education. Here is a little background about grants.

Grant money is usually a government program. In exchange for specific work, they will provide a fixed dollar amount. The first step to this process is to write the grant application. The procedure involves long detailed descriptions of what will be done and who will be doing the work.

Another way of thinking of this is like a job and a job application. The Government posts a job and a vague description of what they want done. Then people write an application detailing why they are the best person for this job. Then your application goes into the pile with everyone else who has completed the application. Rarely do only a couple of people submit for a grant, usually it is hundreds to thousands of submissions. Then the best qualified is awarded the grant.

Once a grant is awarded, periodic reports need to be submitted to the government agency informing them where you are on the project, and if you are in compliance with their request.

Other things to look for if it is truly a grant: deadline to submit application and date of the final award announcement. If you don't see these elements, it's probably a scam.

According to the Consumer Affairs Web site (www.ConsumerAffairs.com): "the government (any government) does not give money away to individuals . . . If you give him your bank account number, he will soon have your funds in his pocket."

BUSINESSES THAT SELL PRODUCTS

Products are all around you. It's the easiest and the hardest part of the business— what do you want to sell? Check out craft fairs and street fairs for new and unusual products. Keep in mind that you want access to the product. You do not want to invest all your money on inventory—at least not to begin with. Know where to find the product, how long it takes to restock, and when peak times and down periods will be for your business and industry.

At the same time, finding product is the hardest thing in the world because there are thousands of new products out there, and trying to find something that's new and profitable may take a long time.

Here are several places and methods where you can find products without emptying your wallet.

Manufactured Items

The easiest way to find products is to go directly to the manufacturer. The library's reference section contains the Thomas Register (www.ThomasRegister.com), which lists manufacturers. Contact the manufacturer regarding the purchasing of products.

The hard part about the Thomas Register is understanding the S.I.C. codes (Standard Industry Classifications). Once you figure out the S.I.C. code in which your manufacturer is located, it becomes easier. That's why we recommend going to the library and talking to the reference librarian the first time.

The new standard is now the North American Industry Classification System (NAICS). Also check out either www.PowerSourcing.com and www.WorldBid.com for additional contacts.

When talking with a manufacturer, there are two reasons why they might not deal with you. First, the overall quantities involved may be either too small or too large. If that's the case, ask for a referral. The manufacturing industry, once you get in the door, is small. Manufacturers know the capacities of other manufacturers.

The other reason a manufacturer might not sell to you is because the manufacturer has an exclusive relationship with someone else. In that case, ask for the name of that company or individual (sales reps, agents or distributors) and deal with them.

Read the contract! In a new working relationship, the contract is the document that both sides will refer to if there is a disagreement. Understand what it says before you sign it. If you are uncomfortable about reviewing the contract yourself, contact us about Pre-Paid Legal Services , as this is one of the services they offer.

From time to time, you may need an attorney to guide you through the many and varying aspects of your business. We used a Pre-Paid Legal Services service, which costs approximately $35 per month. This gives you access to an attorney when you need it without breaking the bank. This is a great solution for the start-up, home-based, mail order and Internet business. One of their services is that they will review contracts. Contact us about Pre-Paid Legal Services as this is one of the many services that is covered with your services.

If you want to export to other countries on a large scale (not just fulfilling an order or two a month), contact the Department of Commerce (www.DOC.gov) 202-637-3077. Many years ago, one of the author's, Mike, took an excellent seminar sponsored by the Department of Commerce.

Check your local community colleges and universities for seminars (one session long— not a quarter or semester class). Also, check your local library for books on the subject.

If the products are manufactured outside the United States, contact the Trade and Economic Development Councils or their consulates. These councils have lists of companies interested in doing business in the United States.

Trade Shows

Since lifestyles and products change rapidly, it's important to get a feel for a particular industry by attending the trade shows, and keeping a lookout for new products to sell.

Call your local (or within driving distance) convention center or mart (jewelry, clothing, and flower) and ask that they send you a list of the upcoming trade shows. The convention center may have this information on its Web site. Once you have found the appropriate trade show, contact the trade show coordinator and ask if it is open to the public. If not, you might like to inquire about becoming a member.

The library's reference section contains *Trade Shows Worldwide*. This directory is cross-referenced by products and industries. You can also check out this Web site www.EventsEye.com. Reference the Encyclopedia of Associations (US) or the National Trade and Professional Associations (**NTPA**), as trade shows are often sponsored by an association. These publications are not on-line.

Many conferences and trade shows offer special workshops, seminars or training before or during or after the show that you may want to take advantage of.

Closeouts

There are firms that supply surplus merchandise from discontinued stock (closeouts). Depending on the industry, *closeouts* can have slightly different meanings.

In the garment industry where there are five seasons (winter, spring, summer, fall and Christmas), closeouts can mean merchandise from the previous season. There is nothing wrong with either the garment or the manufacturer. Large chain stores may require minimum quantities when handling the garment and if the number falls below the minimum, the garment is moved out.

In the electronics industry, technology is redesigned about every 9-18 months. With software and computers, technology turnover is even shorter. Closeouts might occur when the new, smaller, and faster equipment is introduced into the market.

When buying closeouts from a manufacturer that is going out of business or is no longer manufacturing the products (nor supporting the warranties), then your advertising should state that there are no exchanges or returns. A wise rule of thumb would be to maintain a minimum quantity internally just for parts, pieces, and replacements.

Interested in liquidation bargains? Go to www.Liquidation.com for products being liquidated.

Another interesting method of getting mechanize is to bid on a storage unit where people have stopped paying their fee. When the individual storage unit goes up for auction, you cannot inspect the items. You stand outside the unit and look inside.

You are bidding blind. Most of the items are old clothes, worn-out furniture, and paper. Go to www.Auctioneers.org (National Auctioneers Association) Web site (or a similar site) and see what auctions are coming up. When we researched this site, Walmart Used Asset Division was auctioning items. Also check out www.Govdeals.com for deals.

Consignment

Consignment means that the manufacturer lends the merchandise to you for a period of time without payment. At the end of the predefined and agreed upon period (120 days for instance), either the unsold merchandise is returned or payment is made for sold merchandise.

Examples of goods often sold on consignment include light bulbs, produce, eggs, poultry, magazines, newspapers, Christmas decorations, garden seeds, batteries for flashlights and potted plants found in supermarkets.

Bookstores have been using this method for years, although they don't call it consignment. Bookstores have a 100 percent return policy with the publisher (manufacturer). The publisher pays for shipping to the bookstore and from the bookstore back to the warehouse. Perhaps you have seen this notice in the front of a paperback book:

> **NOTE:** If you purchased this book without a cover you should be aware that this book is stolen property. It was reported as "unsold and destroyed" to the publisher, and neither the author nor the publisher has received any payment for this "stripped book."

Instead of shipping the whole book back and incurring more expense on a non-sold product, the publisher has agreed to credit a returned book when only the cover has been returned.

If you want to have your product on consignment in a store or boutique because the proprietor is not interested in buying your product, contact the purchasing department. Inquire about their policy regarding consignment programs. Consignment selling to a retail store is the same as open purchase order selling with the exception of the consignment agreement.

Although you may be excited about getting your product into the store, the following points should be discussed:

- Placement: where are your products going to be placed? You don't want them stuck where customers won't see them. The most sought after location is near the checkout counter, but don't expect that. Place your products where it would be exposed to an estimated 50 percent of foot traffic. As customers enter the store would be good.

- Length of time: will the store have 30 days to sell your product or 365 days? What can you live with and follow up on in a timely manner?

- Damaged goods: do you want the damaged product back? Yes, you do! Although you don't necessarily want to keep tabs on the store (saying that it was damaged when in truth they sold it), you do want to do a product evaluation. Did the packaging stand up to normal wear and tear? Are you seeing consistent problems which could be addressed and fixed?

Drop Shipment

This method cuts inventory overhead because there is little or no inventory. You still have product to sell. You advertised the product. The customer orders from you. The customer's order and address, along with the wholesale payment, are sent to the drop shipment firm. The manufacturer ships the order directly to the customer.

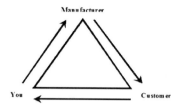

Internet and faxes have made drop shipment arrangements easy. When the economy is tough, more manufacturers are willing to drop ship. When the economy is good, manufacturers are less willing to develop new drop ship relationships. It never hurts to ask.

Here is a company (ABS) that does business with us. We drop ship the product to its customer. Notice the system that has been put in place.

*** WARNING *** WARNING *** WARNING *** WARNING *** WARNING ***

We must know the status of every order!

Part of the agreement that you have with ABS is to fulfill orders that are sent to you *quickly* - and to *confirm shipment*. The methods to *confirm shipment*, in order of preference, are:

* E-mail: Sales@theAlternativeBookShop.com
* Fax: (727) 399-0442
* Phone: (727) 399-0342
* Mail: ABS, 250 176th Avenue East, Redington Shores, FL 33708-1221

Confirmations should simply include the title, B.P. # from the Book Payment form, and date & method of shipment.

Failure to comply with this procedure may result in removal of your book from ABS

A variation on this technique is the advertising agent where the customer sees the ad you placed and orders directly from the manufacturer. Each advertisement order form is coded with your code number, from which a commission is paid to you on each item sold.

Another variation of this is Amazon.com. The triangle relationship is the customer, Amazon and you. You list your books on Amazon's *Available from these sellers*. The customer goes to Amazon and find the book, DVD or CD that they are looking for. Then the customer has the option of purchasing from the alternative sellers. The customer pays Amazon. Amazon notifies the seller of the order and shipping address. At the end of the month, the seller gets a check from Amazon.

SMC Specialty Merchandise offers drop shipment. You can contact them at www.SMCorp.com or 818-998-3300. You may remember the late night commercials of SMC with their spokesman Tom Bosley many, many years ago.

Do an internet search for drop ship manufacturers and do YOUR research of companies and products you would be interested in selling.

With consignment or drop shipment, the risks are lower because there is little or no inventory, and no warehouses full of unsold merchandise.

Cafepress.com

This is an interesting middle ground between having your own product and buying existing products from your own source. Let's say that you have a trademark. We're going to use Nancy's Clutterology trademark for this example.

The clutter bug would be great on a mug, so we go to www.Cafepress.com and establish an account, providing our trademark in download form and giving them our credit card number.

Back on our Web site, www.Clutterology.com we have the cute clutter bug mug for sale. The customer clicks on the order and Cafepress makes one mug and ships it to our customer (drop ship). Check Cafepress's Web site and see what products they have that would be good to sell on your Web site. We have no inventory and per unit price is pretty reasonable.

The categories they have are: t-shirts and clothing; home and gifts; cards and stationery; art and posters; signs and fun stuff; books and CDs.

CHAPTER 4 CREATING AN EFFECTIVE BUSINESS WEB SITE

Your Web site is your four-color catalog. Its purpose is to make money for you—not to give your money to the Web site designer. Studies have shown that buyers who do not want or need to have the physical experience of the product prior to purchase are prime candidates for electronic catalog shopping.

The Web reduces the cost of creating and storing hundreds of pages of information to only pennies per day. You can direct your potential customers to your Web sites to view your electronic brochures in a fraction of the time, and from there to an electronic shopping cart to place orders.

There are a few key things to consider before you construct your site:

1. The Web is a gigantic library that customers can access for free—anytime they want to use it. Your Web site is like having a book in this library. Your home page is the cover of your book. This means that you can supply your advertising materials, plus lots of other stuff for FREE. This is the only reason you need to justify having a Web site!

2. Your Web site is the electronic equivalent of a four-color catalog. Just because you can write and electronically print a lot of material at no additional charge doesn't mean you should. Your customers are time-constrained, and getting to the heart of what you have to say will assist them in getting and applying your information. Start to collect catalogs to generate ideas for your Web site. Is the front cover (home page) interesting? Is the order form (shopping cart) easy to understand? Are the items layout in an appearing way (interior pages)?

3. Your Web site is being created for the benefit of the customer, not for your own personal enjoyment or entertainment. Keep all the fancy graphics, animated cartoons, and other distracting elements off the site unless they are a critical part of the information.

Your Web site doesn't have to be fancy or exotic. It does have to be effective. Most Web site development software comes with templates that create a basic outline of the site for you. All you have to do is fill in the contents for the customer. You are not in a Web site or graphics design contest. The purpose of your Web site is to give customers the information they need to either make a decision or to educate themselves about you.

If the Web site is the equivalent to a catalog, here are some suggestions on how to layout and design your Web site catalog.

1. Think like a cataloger, not like a retailer. You are not selling face to face. Customers cannot ask questions, so anticipate their questions and supply the answers in the catalog. Use a *refer a friend* link.

2. Keep the order form simple. Include all the needed information. Ask for names of friends who would like to get the catalog.

3. Spell out the return policy, payment methods accepted, delivery times, sales tax, and shipping charges. Print the telephone number in large type on each page or spread.

4. Make sure the headlines are attention-grabbers that appeal to the customer's self-interest.

5. Put a date on the catalog to avoid confusion when another catalog is sent later.

6. Offer discounts for multiple orders. It works, and so do guarantees. They are often the deciding factor for uncertain catalog shoppers.

7. Include the address of the retail location, if there is one. Catalogs often drive retail sales.

8. Include sizing information if it's needed.

9. When fulfilling orders, include a related product sales piece to generate future sales.

10. Offer overnight delivery for an extra charge. People use catalogs for convenience.

"Designers design, they do not know what attracts people."
So you need to guide your designer."
Bill Brooks
March 9, 2002 NSA/GLAC meeting

WEB DESIGNERS MYTHS

When you approach your web designer, you may want to put all your trust in that person. Don't. As the business owner, your web site must sell. Avoid they myths that your designers spouts.

H.I.T.S.

Since the birth of the Internet, the word *hits* is often used. If you were interviewing a Web site designer, they would extol their virtues and talk about how many hits a Web site gets because of their phenomenal colors, layout, graphics, spinning beer bottles, and so forth. With the dot.com explosion, for the first time in history labor told management how to run their companies.

Web site designers will often say that the greater the number of hits, the greater the exposure the Web site gets. Mike has a standard reply for that comment when organizations ask him to speak for them but are unable to pay for his full speaking fee. The conversation goes like this:

"Mike, we would like you to speak for the ABC organization but we are unable to pay for your full speaking fee. However, the ABC organization is such a great organization that we will give you a great deal of exposure!"

"Uhm, let me think about that. You are unable to pay for my speaking fee, so you want to expose me to more people that can't afford my services either. No, I think I'll pass."

When you hear the word *hits*, translate it into the acronym h.i.t.s. or How Idiots Track Success. Hits have little to do with the success of your business. They are a good starting point, just like the number of newspapers printed, audited subscribers of a magazine, and drive-by traffic for a storefront. If you cannot get people to take the next step (call, write, inquire, and stop in) you won't be in business long.

Here is a great example of a Web designer's great idea for getting hits gone bust.

If you were planning a trip to Washington DC and wanted to take a tour of the White House, most people would type in www.WhiteHouse.com without thinking. Dot com is the most common extension. However, the site that you should go to for tours of the White House is www.WhiteHouse.gov. The idea of using .com was to capitalize on people not thinking.

The .com site was an adult entertainment site. When kids discovered that WhiteHouse.com was an adult site, the information spread like wild fire. Every school and library had to block the .com site to prevent kids from entering the site.

The important question to make this scheme work is what do people wanting a tour of the White House and a porn site have in common. Nothing. The site had tons of hits, but few sales. Since that time it has changed many times in the past couple of years.

BLOGS

You must have a BLOG (WE**B LOG**). For all practical purposes this is a big bulletin board that allows customers to leave any messages, pictures, videos, audios, or material they feel is related to the site's purpose.

Our definition of a BLOG is "dear diary, today I did . . ." The question that you need to ask regardless of what your Web designers says, "Will a BLOG bring me more business"?

Before you decide to BLOG, be sure that it is advantageous to you and to your business before you decide to create one. Apply Rule #1—ask yourself is that expenditure (of time and money) will make a difference between the customer ordering and not ordering?

Something else to remember is that most BLOGs are usually opinions rather than facts. Donny Deutsch in one of his programs suggested that you get bloggers to talk about you—great a buzz about you!

For more information about blogs go to www.Bobology.com. Bob Cohen frequently teaches several classes at the community colleges.

Search Engines

You have to do this and that to get to the top of the search engines. Most people don't know how to use a search engine or how to find what they are looking for. Providing a massive list of meta-tags (index words) will help somewhat. The best way to get people to your Web site is to use conventional advertising to get your URL in their hands so they can go directly to your site.

Rule #2: Speed costs, so asking yourself how fast you want to go now applies to search engine listing and has given rise to a specialized service called Search Engine Listing and Optimization. If you want your site to be listed rapidly and to control the content and listing hierarchy, you will have to invest both time and money to get listed with the major engines.

The two possible exceptions are DMOZ http://dmoz.org and Google www.Google.com where you can still add your URL for free.

If search engine positioning is critical to your success, the best answer is to use a firm that specializes in search engine optimization such as Attach USA (www.AttachUSA.com). Search engine optimization firms have a staff of professionals who monitor and understand what is required for proper positioning and listing with the engines.

Graphics

You need sexy looking graphics. The Web is magnificent for its ability to display almost any kind of graphics. For that reason graphics have become a dominant element in the world of advertising.

Fifty-eight percent of the homes have Internet service. It is estimated that this is where it will top out at. Many people work at a computer all day and the last thing that they want to do at home is work on the computer. Statistics show that 50 percent of the Web's home users are still using POTS lines (Plain Old Telephone Service with 28.8 or 56k modems).

Although there are a variety of considerations when using graphics on your Web site, the most important considerations are:

1. Your home page should download in less than 10 seconds with a 28.8 modem so the customer does not get aggravated and click you off. (If you need high-resolution graphics, use thumbnail graphics so that customers don't have to endure the long download times waiting for them to load.)

2. Is it necessary? Each graphic takes time to download, and excessive download times may aggravate customers to the point where they click off your site and go somewhere else. Graphics and other large files take a long time to download when using a modem.

3. Have the graphics and content been optimized for the customer's computer system? High-resolution graphics might work well on your computer, but the customer may have a lower resolution system making your Web site a blur or creating an oversize image on their monitor. Although there have been several attempts at a universal scaling software package, the results have been less than satisfactory so if you're concerned about optimal viewing when someone visits your Web site, you'll need to create a user selectable variety of duplicate pages with varying resolution and complexity so they can choose the optimal version for their needs.

   There is a *do-it-yourself* software patch that automatically detects an iPod Touch or and iPhone and will rescale the graphics and site content to the correct size. It's free www.EngageInteractive.co.uk/blog/2008/06/19/tutorial-building-a-website-for-the-iphone/#detection.

4. Have you used thumbnails and JPEG graphics wherever possible? JPEG pictures have about 40 percent less resolution and clarity than GIF. However, they download in about one-third the time. Thumbnails are small, low-resolution pictures that can be linked to bigger, high-resolution pictures if necessary.

Sound and Video

The more sound and video you have on your web site the better. Known as multimedia, sound and video can be added to a Web site to enhance its appeal to the customer. It can create exciting infomercials for products and services that are dynamic rather than static. Interactive video, full color, multimedia sound, and easy access are making this more attractive to both suppliers and consumers.

The most versatile and widely distributed FREE software programs for adding multimedia is Microsoft's Windows Media Player for free www.Microsoft.com/windows/windowsmedia/player/11/default.aspx.

MISTAKES TO AVOID

You have taken all that time to create the web site, but is it a tool for your customer, or is it all about you? Is it helping you or hurting you. Do you actually have a web presence? Have you updated your web site since the first time you published it? Are you exploring social networking? As you still using AOL.com or Earthlink.net or gmail.com for your e-mail instead of your website URL domain presense?

Call To Action

Many times the Web site forgets the call to action. What do you want people to do? It's not that people are stupid it's that they don't have time to think what the next step is—so tell them.

For our small business, we cannot afford to wait around for a customer to someday buy from us. We need their money now, today, this week, this month, or this quarter.

Don't be shy, be bold! *Call, write, e-mail,* or *stop by* are all calls to actions. Can you make *your* call to action a little stronger? Use a deadline. Create a sense of urgency.

Other typical calls to action are:

1. Call our toll free number within the next hour and receive _____.

2. Offer expires _____.

3. Visit our Web site before _____ for a free bonus.

4. Visit our Web site to buy now.

5. Visit our Web site to learn more

6. Visit our Web site Save!!

7. Click here to _____.

8. Please Retweet Me!

Put an aura of timeliness to it: *Prices guaranteed through Midnight Saturday night. Offer expires June 31, 2015.* Make sure that people order **now**. What happens if they order July 1? Well, the 50 percent reduction is guaranteed only through the end of June so act now . . . .

When using the *visit our Web site,* be specific. It is not enough of an incentive for most people to just visit your Web site. Make the offer compelling.

Other great words to use are: call today, get involved, and shop now for the best selection.

Tell Them

People don't always know what your product is, how to use your product or what to do with your product. Most people don't have time to think. So, your job is to spoon feed the information to them until they say, "Eureka, that's just what I need!"

We love a Jack in the Box tray liner for Jack Cash Card. Instead of just saying, "Buy the card," they list 52 holidays when the card would make a great gift. Besides the standard holidays like Christmas, Halloween, and Easter are some less known (celebrated) holidays like Arbor Day, National Sibling Day, and National Nut Day.

When you have read all 52 holidays, you mind may say something like, "oh, hey, Dad's birthday is coming up." "I haven't seen Aunt Rita, I should get ..."

Below is another great example of a call to action. Rosemary is a charity and instead of saying, "We need you" they tell you specifically how you can help. When you finish reading this, you may say to yourself, "Hey I have wrapping paper in my closet with a couple unused backpacks." Things you won't have thought of by yourself if they charity had just said, "send money!"

Sweeten the Deal

> Buy 2 get 50% off
>
> Buy 1 for $19.99; 2nd for 1¢
>
> Buy 1 get 1 FREE!

There is a 40 percent higher response rate to *buy 1 get 1 free* because of the word FREE!

If possible, add a free gift to your offer. In the English language, this is grammatically redundant because a gift is free. From an advertising point of view, three times as many people will respond to a *free gift* compared to a gift.

If you are providing a service, be sure to let your customer know what additional service you have given for free. Did you underestimate how long the project would take? On your invoice state:

5 hours of additional work .... No Charge (NC)

There is a book called *The Tipping Point* by Malcolm Gladwell; which documents why and how when using buy one get one free isn't more expensive than the other two.

According to the *Cheapskate Monthly*, December 2001 (www.CheapSkateMonthly.com), numerical signs such as "Two for the price of one or Limited three per person, cause shoppers to buy 30 to 90 percent more than they otherwise would. This happens even if the item isn't on sale." So to increase sales, you may want to limit the number of items with a specific offer.

During the 2009 Super Bowl, Denny's ran an ad for a free Grand Slam breakfast from 6 AM to 2 PM following the Super Bowl. Estimates were that they spent three million dollars on airtime (excluding production and talent costs), and gave away two million breakfasts at $5.99 each.

They received over 50 million dollars in news coverage and their Web site had so many hits that it was occasionally down. The best part (the way Denny's made money) of this is that most people would go to Denny's with a friend. We would guess that only 50 percent would order the Grand Slam breakfast (generating revenue). Also, this campaign got people back to Denny's.

LAYOUT OF WEB SITE

Obviously, since this is the electronic equivalent of a catalog, you can place anything on the Web site that makes sense for your marketing needs. Let's examine the specifics of what is available to you and why you might or might not want to include it in your site.

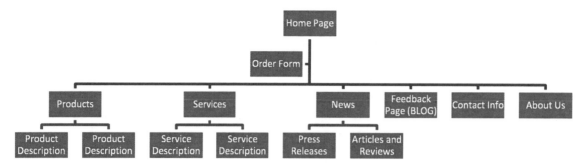

"The American Library Association indicates that we have three main reading groups today: 10-15 percent are non-readers (which includes functionally illiterate), 10-15 percent are avid readers (which intently read everything from the small print on the cereal box—even if they read it the morning before, to the newspaper from front to back); and 70-80 percent are skimmers (browsing and scanning their way along)."

How does this apply to us? We must accommodate all three groups, because they all have money to spend and hopefully they will spend it with us!

For non-readers, you should include pictures to deliver your message. Include a picture of the product in your copy. As a fallback position on your order form on the Internet, guide non-readers along by using: #1, #2 . . . This will help them in the order process.

The best way to attract the non-readers and skimmers into your piece is with photographs, clip art illustrations, and color. Non-readers will call the telephone numbers listed for more information and verbally inquire if interested.

Long body text is designed for avid readers. Jay Abraham and Gary Halbert are two copywriters who specialize in long body copy. You have probably seen their work—in the mail comes a 12-14 page letter with few pictures, lots of underlined words, and a PS at the end of the letter plus a PPS. Avid readers require details, facts, statistics, directions, fine print, credibility, and testimonials or endorsements from others.

Skimmers like bullets, short paragraphs (about three sentences in length), and lots of white space. They appreciate short body copy, subheads, and bullet points highlighting the benefits and features of the product, service, or event.

A short, above the fold (one screen page) message may produce results for you. Do you remember when the newspaper was delivered and dropped on your front door? The most important news was on the front page. The big news was placed above the fold so that it was the first item you saw in the newspaper.

The Web gives us a wonderful option for those who want written information because we can start with short copy or bullet points. For those who want more, the Web gives the option to click for medium or detailed copy, specifications, and long reports if needed.

Home Page

Access to a Web site starts with the home page. It is called the home page to indicate its role as a starting point. Although it looks exactly the same as any Web page, its operation is radically different. The home page contains the URL (Universal Resource

Locator) or address of the site plus hidden key or profile words search engines use to find your Web site.

From the home page, customers can access other sources of information by clicking on text or symbols that have been predesignated as a link point. The text that will link to other material (hypertext links) is different from other text in that it is usually shown in a different color and is underlined (for example www.RoundsMiller.com).

Think of the home page as the cover of your book, or the entry point into your catalog. Although you can make it as fanciful and animated as your imagination will allow, the time to download it onto a customer's computer, coupled with its appropriateness to the material contained within the site, becomes a prime consideration in the design.

Ideally, the home page should download in ten seconds or less when the customer is using a 28.8 kbps modem. Most of the better Web site authoring software programs contains download estimators that show what happens to the download time with the addition of each piece of text or graphics.

The home page should include:

Table of Contents

If your site is search enabled (which it should be if it has more than a few pages), make sure there is a search box on the home page.

Since the customer cannot flip through the pages of a Web site like they can through a catalog, it becomes essential that you make it as easy as possible for them to find what they are looking for.

There are two effective approaches to this requirement:

1. An alphabetized and hyperlinked table of contents where customers can look up what they want and click on the link. This will automatically connect them to the item. An easy-to-use linked table of contents on the home page is a must to make sure the customer can find what he or she is looking for—fast. (Put it in the margins so the customer can get to it from anywhere inside the site!)

2. A site search engine allows customers the opportunity to type what they know into a box and let the engine find it for them. Some customers don't want to look things up alphabetically, or they may have a key word in a description of an item rather than its proper title.

Make the layout logical and simple to navigate. Customers are there to gather information, not to get lost exploring a labyrinth. If you think the customer may want or need more information, write short pages to begin with and then link them to longer copy as an option.

Page Title

The browser window should display your site's title and a brief description. Use language that will be informative in bookmark lists and search engines.

Logo and Tagline

Include your company name and/or logo in its expected location—the top left hand corner of the page. Use your logo on every page. It's the continuity the customer sees. It's your branding. Identify what your site is all about, preferably in a one-sentence tagline. Don't let anyone wonder what you do or what you sell. For a service company, this could be a variation on your elevator story.

Contact Information

Contact information must be easy to find. If possible, include it on every page of your site. This includes name, address, telephone, fax, 800 or toll free telephone number, customer service hours, and e-mail.

Don't hide from your customers. Some people do need to contact you by phone or are curious about what city you are located in. It doesn't mean that they will show up at your door step. Many times, a Web site is judge if it is legitimate or just a scam when people check the contact information. The less information that's there, the more you are hiding. The more that you are hiding, the more distrusted you become.

Copyright Notice

It's often advantageous to post the copyright notice on the home page to advise customers that the site's contents are proprietary and not to be copied or used without your specific written permission. This issue can become critical if you are publishing tips, insights, articles, or other information that might be copied by customers and reprinted as their own.

External Links

If there are resources, either internally on your site or externally on others sites—such as maps, driving directions, or times and places of related events—you feel will be of interest to customers, make it easy for people to access them by creating hyperlinks.

Webmaster

If there is a problem with a site (suggestions, correction and broken links), customers will usually pass it along to the person designated as the site designer (Webmaster). This link automatically activates the Webmaster's e-mail.

Last Date Updated

With the sheer tonnage of information available on today's Web, many customers look at the last date updated to see if there have been any changes in the site since their last visit.

Sign In and Sign Up

If your site requires users to log in for access, make the log in area prominent on the home page. If you plan to solicit user e-mail addresses for a newsletter or other communication, ask for the sign up on every page, including the home page.

Additional Types of Pages

The number and style of pages are endless. Here are a few others you may want to consider.

Product and/or Service Page

This is what will interest most people with buying power (money). Since the Web site has almost unlimited capability (at virtually no cost) to create and display descriptions, specifications, applications, and other pertinent details of what you are offering, this is the perfect place to do it. There are a variety of ways to list and link these descriptions. The cleanest is to list each product or service and then link it to a page that contains short (less than 100 words), medium (between 100 and 250 words), and long (more than 500 words) descriptions about the item.

When you present the information in this manner, you give customers an active choice of how much (or how little) they need in order to get enough information to make a decision about the product or service.

Pictures (Low-Resolution)

If there is a reason why the Web's popularity exploded over the old text system, it has to be graphics and color. Digital photography has made it simple and inexpensive to provide full color images of goods. Services that demonstrate to the customer the appearance and functions of what you are offering can be either photos or video.

If you have bought or sold something on eBay, you know the importance of the picture. When the image is available, the product sells better than an auction without an image. People will look at the image and may not even read the description.

FAQ's Page

This page anticipates the **f**requently **a**sked **q**uestions a person might have about your products or services. It helps eliminate the phone calls or e-mails that become repetitive so you can concentrate on getting and handling more business.

What's New Page

Your business is a dynamic (changing) entity, and customers may be interested to know what is new, what you have been working on, what you have accomplished, and what your future plans are all about.

Don't make the customers hunt throughout the entire site to see what's new and different. Put a special index page on your site with links so that customers can immediately see what has been changed without the frustration of having to browse the entire site.

PR or Media Page

When you do something new and different, it's a good idea to put out a press release. If you have ever had any experience with press releases, you know they are printed as editor's choice material because you don't pay for the space. The end result is that most releases do not get printed.

Your Web site is another story because it's yours. You can post press releases about what you have done and what you are going to do in a positive, sensational manner.

For selling your services, this is where background information, industry information, and commercial viability of information articles are placed.

Privacy Policy

If you collect any information from your users, have a clearly written and easily found Privacy Policy. Search the Internet for *sample privacy policy*. The BBB Online has a good example for your to work from.

Reviews and Articles Page

Whenever you receive any kind of written review (especially if it is positive) you should immediately obtain reprint rights and post it on your Web site. These serve as testimonials. Since they are written by an independent party (such as a magazine or newspaper) they are perceived as being unbiased.

There are two types of articles, those written about you and those written by you. The articles written by you would include tips and ideas to help people.

Hidden Pages

There are a lot of things to which you want only selected people to have access and this is where we put them. (NOTE: These pages should NEVER have a link ANYWHERE on the site! The only way a customer should know they exist is because you have given them the URL.) These include notes and handouts, material developed for a specific group rather than for public, or a special offer that's only being made available to selected customers.

Another popular use of these pages is for material (an e-book) that is sold and can only be accessed by people who have been given the exact URL. Other items include maps with driving directions to home offices, price lists, customer interaction documents, and other proprietary information.

Mission Statement Page and About Us Page

Frequently people want to know your philosophy. Create a page for this information. Customers may want to know who you are and why they should trust you. An About Us page is the expected place to give this information.

Autoresponders

One of the earliest marketing tools of the Internet was the autoresponder or MailBot. This ingenious tool is the ONLY device on the Internet that automatically captures customers' mailing information without their having to input data.

Autoresponders gratify customers by sending an e-mail message containing the information that the customer immediately and without additional labor.

You can get your own free autoresponders at www.GetResponse.com and program them to deliver materials to the respondent and, at the same time, capture their e-mail address. Once you have the respondent on a qualified e-mail list, you can create and deliver highly targeted material at virtually no cost.

These fully automated systems deliver information instantly to your prospects, and then can automatically follow up with personalized messages any number of times over the coming days, weeks, or months.

HIRING A WEB DESIGNER

If you decide to hire someone to create your Web site, our suggestion is that you have someone create your **homepage**, a couple of **interior pages** and the **shopping cart**. Most people know how to use a keyboard so inputting and creating the other pages is just a matter of typing it in.

There are several different Web sites that provide Web designers.

Register and post your project: someone creates a homepage, a couple of interior pages and the shopping cart. If you are uncomfortable working with someone from a foreign country, you can exclude them. You will get replies from different freelancers and they will quote you their price. They have samples and a portfolio to view their work, a résumé and feedback from people that have used them. Go to www.Elance.com.

If you go to www.99Designs.com you post a price. For instance: need a Web site created for $100. You will get a variety of replies ranging from just the home page to the complete Web site for that fixed price.

If you want a free Web site for your business (free means it will include advertising for the company that gives you the Web site) go to www.FreeWebs.com and follow their instructions for creating a free Web site.

> *"Technology is like any tool. Magical in the hands of a master.*
> *Ordinary for those that are not willing to study, practice and learn."*
> *Chris Clarke-Epstein*
> *2000-2001 president of the National Speakers Association*

The Web is a powerful business tool! Use it as a business tool to work with your business systems. Expect that the Web is the only thing necessary; you will be sorely disappointed and perhaps even end up broke.

CHAPTER 5 SELLING ON eBAY

There are some people that only sell their product on eBay. Nancy grew up going to auctions. The first Sunday of the month, her dad and brother would go to the horse auction. Before the auction of the animals, there was the auction of the accessories. Nancy sat through a lot of hours anxious about getting a new brush or curry comb. Her dad was cool and non-emotional. His hobby was going to auctions. Guess some of that gene rubbed off on Nancy.

A great place to find products to sell is on eBay. We have even heard of people who buy product from eBay and then resell it on eBay. In August 2008, eBay announced that it would be shifting from online auction towards fixed price resellers. In 2005, 181 million registered users traded more than $44.3 billion in gross merchandise. Nancy does most of her consumer shopping on eBay because she hates to go to a shopping center.

If you want more information about how to sell on eBay, go to the library and check out a book on how to sell on eBay; or attend a class.

If you are planning to use eBay to sell your product, here are a few tips.

Know what you are doing. In other words start to watch auctions before you start to sell. What is the price range for similar products? How often do the products go unsold or are there only one or two bids? What do you like about other people's description? What don't you like about other people's description? EBay has wonderful tutorials that are just a few minutes long. Go to http://pages.ebay.com/education/selling.html to start your education.

The USPS offers free seminars to learn everything you need to know to buy and sell online. From taking pictures of merchandise to closing the deal and getting merchandise delivered—it's all covered. It also includes online shipping solutions offered by the Postal Service. Call your local Post Office

Categories

Getting started on eBay is so easy. You start out by selecting the category. After that point, eBay is a template and you just answer their questions or click on the option. It's about that easy.

One of the first things you will do is select what category to list the item. It has been our experience that categories aren't that helpful to the buyer. Usually the buyer creates a search to find a specific item. Likewise, selecting a second or third category hasn't produced more bids. However, if your items are truly collectibles that fall into a category where buyers look at all the items in that category, select the category carefully.

To start to sell your item, you must start by selecting the category the item will be sold under. When you select the category you simply answer the questions. These are templates which include the most common information. Different categories have slightly different information.

If you have books to sell, this is one of the easiest things to list on eBay. Select the category of BOOKS then the sub-category (children's books; cookbooks; fiction books; magazine back issues; nonfiction books; textbooks; other). Then you are prompted for the ISBN. With that information, almost everything is filled in for you. The size of the book, the publisher and the number of pages. You don't even have to take a picture because that is already associated with the ISBN. How easy is that!

Fees

What will it cost you? The title is free and if you add a subtitle it's $0.50. If the starting price of an auction is $0.01 to $0.99 the fee is $0.10. Final value (selling price) of $0.01 to $25 fee is 8.75 percent.

You will notice that eBay doesn't include shipping and handling cost in calculating their fees. That may be a reason why sellers shipping costs are higher than *normal.*

If you create an eBay Store, the fees are less and the inputting of the products is faster and simpler.

Photographs

Take good pictures. This is probably the most important element. Not many products get sold without pictures. If the same product has two auctions, the one with the better picture will more than likely be the one a buyer would bid on. Digital cameras make it easy but be sure that the picture is clear; there are no shadows, that there is enough light on the product to see it and that any background is not distracting.

If you go to www.ShopGetOrganized.com they have an EBAY PHOTO STUDIO. This is a home photo studio for online auction selling. Includes a light box with an integrated diffuser screen, camera tripod, and two backdrops for light and dark objects ($30). Deluxe model includes two high-output lights with adjustable legs. Backdrop folds into carrying case for easy transport and storage ($59). Item #27699.

Description

Start with a good headline (title). Look what other people call the product. In the advance search criteria, a buyer can search *include title and description.* Most people don't use the advance search feature. What is also amazing is the number of misspellings. You may want to research what common misspellings are and use them in your description so that the customer who misspelled a word in your description can find you. Be sure that you haven't accidently misspelled something in your description!

Create a catchy line for the description and have a good write up. You are competing with gazillions of other vendors. Let people know if you have the manual (or tell them where they can get it online). The more information the better, the more detail the better. If there are any blemishes on the product, let them know. Many times they won't care—if they know about it. However, after they get the product and it's not perfect, people get upset.

When you are a first time seller, you aren't going to have any feedback. In your description, tell people that you are a first time seller. If they have any questions, suggest that they contact you if you left anything out. People like to help, let them.

Mike allowed Nancy to sell some silver spoons that were his mothers. Nancy doesn't know anything about antique or collectible spoons. The description was the information on the back of the spoon with several pictures. There was a statement in the description that if you have any questions, contact the seller. These spoons were inherited and as a first time seller, she didn't know what information the buyer needs.

In the past, there has been some problems with people not paying for the item that they won. What is now typical is that payment must be received within seven days.

Most of the information that you need in this area is already designed by eBay and all you have to do when listing the item is to click on the appropriate box.

One of the neat things is a postal calculator (which you just select and it's added to your description). If you are sending out the product USPS (United States Postal Service), the buyer enters the ZIP code and the cost for postage is calculated.

Most of our products are packed with boxes and packing materials shipped to us. On the more expensive items, we take them to the local mailing store and have the professional pack it. Retailers like Target and Walmart have used boxes in all shapes and sizes and will give them to you for free. Call ahead of time to see what day they unload and have boxes.

State what your return policy is. Our policy is if the item is damaged in shipping, when the item is returned, we'll refund the money. If the item is not to their liking, we don't refund the money.

Don't make your return policy long and lengthy. People might think that you are hard to deal with and have inferior products to begin with. Be as clear and concise as possible. If you are selling items from your closet, go to great length to describe every nick and scratch and imperfection of the item to reduce returns.

Starting Price/Bid
What do you want to price your item at? One theory is to start low (like $.01 instead of $10) and get people excited about the bidding. Once someone has bid a couple of times on an item and several bidders start to bid against each other, they may get so involved in the bidding that the price rises to a nice high price (higher than practical— maybe).

The other theory is that there is only going to be one bidder and therefore you would begin the starting price at a reasonable price (like $10 instead of $.01).

Buy It Now is someplace in between the two theories above. The Buy It Now is the price you are willing to sell the item for. An individual might not want to wait for an auction to end. You can start the bid at $.01 but buy it now for $15.

Are you uncertain what price to list the item at and hesitant to just give it away. Create a Reserve. A reserve is a dollar figure that only you know. Let's say that you have great-aunt's china cup. You don't want to just give it away and you don't know what the fair market value is either. By listing the opening bid low ($.01) and creating a Reserve of $20, all bid less than $20 the bidder would see a message that *the reserve has not been met*. By the end of the auction, if the reserve has not been met, you keep the item. If the reserve has been met, then the buyer gets the item. The eBay fee for listing a Reserve is $2.

Because the reserve is not known to the bidder, if the bidder saw $20 as the starting bid may not bid at all. But, when playing the bidding game/war, the price could quickly pass $20.

If you have more than one of the same item, you can sell them on the same auction. Just click on the box.

Length
How long should the auction be? We typically go with the cheapest option. Which is typically the seven day auction. Why add cost to the product when you don't have to? There has been a time when we were going to be out of town when the seven day auction ended, so we selected a shorter auction. Seven day auctions begin the moment you enter the data. You don't select the starting time or day.

A new feature has been when to start the auction. You can set everything up and then start the auctions a couple days later.

Most bidding takes place in the last 12 hours. We might even say the last hour. If this is a truth, the length of the auction is less important than when it ends.

So when should the auction end. If your item is for personal use, most people spend computer/Internet time on the weekend—Sunday evening specifically. Choose a time on Sunday evening that is good for both coasts (East and West Coast time zones).

If your item is a business item, schedule the item to end about 5 PM on Friday night.

International Sales
As strange as it sounds, one of the hottest items on eBay a couple of years ago was piano sales to England. It seems difficult to believe that with shipping costs that it's cheaper to buy at auction, but it was.

One great thing about eBay is that it is international. You may not have traveled to other countries and the idea of shipping something to another country is foreign to you, but don't restrict international sales.

If you are shipping merchandise to another country, be prepared to pass your mail or packages through customs. International mail is subject to customs examination in the destination country. Both the contents and value of an item must be declared on the applicable customs form supplied by the US Government.

You can get the forms and information you need to fill them out correctly at www.USPS.com/international/customs.htm before you send mail to another country.

A trip to your local mailing store is also helpful. They have a wealth of information. The first time you ship internationally, go through your local mailing store, let them pack it. Watch what they do. Watch how much packing material they use, how they label the box and then after that, do it yourself.

Once you start selling items, you will get an idea of what to do and how to do it and it becomes easy.

Buyers Questions

Communicate with buyers. If someone sends you an e-mail wanting more information, details or have any questions, get back to them within 24 hours. "If you are non-responsive during the auction, how long will it take for you to ship the item?" is the question buyers are asking themselves. On higher priced items be sure to make it easy to communicate with you. We have heard of situations where buyers wanted to talk to sellers over the phone. There were just too many questions and details to send e-mails.

Consider adding your phone number to the description. If you are uncomfortable about listing your home phone number, go out a buy a disposable cell phone with minimal minutes.

We have had the bidder's e-mail delivered to us two ways. On the auction item page, there is a button to *Ask seller a question*. Most of the e-mails come into our e-mail system just like a regular old e-mail. Or you can check your *My eBay* and there will also be the same e-mail message.

Disputes

One of the nicest things about eBay is that you are not alone—either as the buyer or seller. If you have any problems, eBay is there to help you. Their Resolution Center is for both buyers and sellers.

Feedback

Although we felt that feedback was important in the beginning, we feel that now it isn't that important. Feedback is still an integral part of eBay. There are sellers that send out e-mails after the auction asking for feedback.

PayPal

EBay and PayPal seem to go together. See the Chapter on Getting People's Money for specifics about PayPal. When you have an auction, PayPal has additional features. Between 60 and 80 percent of the payments for eBay auctions are through PayPal. When the auction is completed, eBay sends you a message about the winning bidder. Then you click on *send an invoice* and because all the information is already there, you don't have to fill in the name of the buyer, the item that was purchased or the winning price. Just click and send it to the buyer.

Unsold Items

If your goes unsold, you can re-list it. EBay has offered it two different ways. If you relist immediately, there is no additional fee. We have had an item that didn't sell the first week and then sold the second week. Other items, we just held until a different time of year. Look in your crystal ball and find out what is best for you.

EBay is constantly updating their site and services. What and how you list an item today might change in three months.

What You Can't Sell

It is true that you can sell almost anything on eBay; however, there are a few things that you can't: bootlegged audio, video, software or computer games. Knockoff fashion designs whether they are clothing or accessories. Alcohol, tobacco and firearms. If you are dealing in these areas, you should be knowledgeable about the rules and regulation in the first place. The FTC prohibits TV descramblers from being sold. Animal and wildlife products that are prohibited in the US. Concert tickets may have restrictions, so check first.

EBay is easy. You don't need a kit or a store to start. Let experience be your teacher. Just get started!

CHAPTER 6 BUSINESS STRUCTURES

There are several types of business structures. They are: sole proprietor, partnership, corporation, nonprofit, and Limited Liability Company. Some of these structures are formed at the county level and some at the state level.

However, just because these are same structures doesn't mean that the IRS recognizes them as the same structure. In other words, you may create a Subchapter S Corporation with your state (corporation), and would file income taxes as an individual with the IRS (sole proprietorship).

SOLE PROPRIETORSHIP

A sole proprietorship is an unincorporated business that is owned by one individual (or a married couple). It is the simplest form of business organization.

For most individuals, a sole proprietorship is the type of business to set up. It's easy and uncomplicated. You are the business and the business is you. Business income and expenses are reported on your personal income taxes.

Guidelines whether to create a sole proprietorship are:

1. You (or your spouse) have very few assets to protect.

2. The type of business you're going into isn't prone to lawsuits.

3. You're not planning to sell the business (when you retire, the business retires).

4. You're not planning to have many (if any) employees.

Sole proprietor files a Schedule C along with the regular 1040 form to report the business income or loss.

You are called an **owner** of a sole proprietorship.

Business Name

What you call your business is not as important as the products you sell. Customers are buying the products, not the name. If you plan to sell the business in the future, the value of the business is higher if the name of the business does not contain your name.

For some people, deciding on the name of their company is easy. For others, giving birth to a child is easier. Here are four things to consider when choosing your company name.

1. Is it possible to include the name of what you are selling in the name of the company?

2. Is the name of your business too broad?

3. Is the name of your business too narrow? If you were to choose another product or service, would the name be outdated? Today, company names with dot com seem to be outdated.

4. Research the name you have in mind using Google or some other search engine. How many other companies have the same name or something close? You want people to remember your name, but you don't want them going to the competition or to another vendor.

Domain Name (URL)

One of the most important aspects of your business, after creating your business name, is to link that business name with your domain name or URL (Universal Resource Locator) on the Internet.

Get a URL (name) for your site that makes sense. It should be uniquely yours and something that people will remember. Do your best to keep it fewer than 15 characters. The longer the URL is, the more possibilities there are for customers to mistype it. If they misspell your URL, they will never find you.

To make your life easier, go to our web site, www.RoundsMiller.com, click onto the Affiliate Services, look for the web site hosting & domain names (either 1 and 1; or Go Daddy). Select either 1and1 or GoDaddy. Either of these web hosting companies are good and have been around for years.

Domain name registration can be accomplished by paying an annual fee to Network Solutions (www.netsol.com), either directly or through a broker/dealer. Go to www.WhoIs.net research the name in a matter of minutes.

High quality, low-cost domain name availability and Web site hosting is at www.GoDaddy.com or www.1and1.com. Each has a search engine that will help you search what is available. You can register the domain name there or shop for a better rate.

The fees range from $2 to $35 per year depending on who is brokering the process. Here are some other sites that offer reduced rates on domain name registration: www.DomainDirect.com, www.enom.com, www.ItsYourDomain.com (is now Hover), www.APlusNet.com, www.Register.com and www.RegSelect.com.

Domain name kidnapping is a practice that occurs when unscrupulous Web site designers seek a way to make additional money from you, or they want to create an insurance policy against you changing designers. This is how it could happen: you request that the Web site developer register your domain name. The request is a valid and sound business practice as long as the developer registers the domain name in your name and passes the registration and billing along to you. When this process is followed, you get to use the domain name and have paid the developer for registering the name.

The problem occurs when the developer registers the name to his organization instead of yours and doesn't tell you. The kidnapping process occurs if you decide to terminate the services of the developer. At this point, the unscrupulous developer will announce that he owns the domain name, then he charges you an exorbitant amount of money (sometimes thousands of dollars) to transfer the registration to you.

The primary problem with domain name kidnapping is that although it's unethical, it isn't technically illegal. To prevent your domain name from being kidnapped, be conscientious and insist that you are the actual registrant for your domain name and that you receive the annual invoices from Network Solutions.

Doing Business As (DBA)—Fictitious Business Name Statement

Names that suggest the existence of additional owners must be registered as fictitious business names. This is also known as filing a DBA (Doing Business As) or a Fictitious Name Statement (FNS). A fictitious name statement is the lowest form of registration. The registration is either accomplished at the county clerk's office or with the secretary of state. Not all counties require a doing business as (fictitious business name) as nor do all states.

At the county level, this is handled by the county clerk, county recorder or country clerk/recorder's office.

The types of business structures that can file a Fictitious Business Name are: an individual, a corporation, a limited partnership, a general partnership, a trust, husband and wife, a limited liability company, and/or state or local registered domestic partners. You can file more than one DBA at a time.

Before you fill out the DBA, here is what you need to know. Who is filing for a DBA, what is the address and in what publication will the DBA be published (you don't have to know the answer at the time of filing but it must be done within 30 days of filing). Typically, send the original and three copies of the form (one certified copy is for the bank, one copy is for the newspaper, and one copy is for your record), a self-addressed stamped envelope to ensure a prompt return of your copies, and payment. You may pay by check (personal, company, bank, or cashiers), money order or traveler's checks.

The county clerk's office is only a repository of fictitious business name statements. They don't research the business name. They don't approve or disapprove the name, or check for similarities or duplications among DBA's. Many states do not have a state-wide database. The filing of a fictitious business name statement does not guarantee exclusive use of that name. Check with the Secretary of State's (California www.ss.ca.gov/business/corp/corporate.htm) to check if there is a corporation with your name or the US Patent and Trademark Office (www.USPTO.gov).

The first part is filing the DBA with the county clerk; the second part is publishing it in a newspaper.

Filing

There are four different ways that you can file a DBA.

1. The simplest way to accomplish the filing of a DBA is to contact your local newspaper. The newspaper has the forms and the knowledge of what needs to be done and how to do it. You fill out the paperwork and the newspaper processes the statement to the county clerk. Check around for the newspaper with the cheapest rates. In our research, we haven't found information about filing a DBA on the newspaper's Web site.

2. Go to the county clerk's office. You may have to pass by some people waiting there. If they offer to give you directions and you say the clerk's office, they will give you the directions and a flyer for publication of the notice in their publication. After you file with the county clerk's office, you must publish the notice in a newspaper.

3. Call the county clerk and ask that the forms be mailed to you. Return the completed statement to the clerk along with the fee for filing the statement. Then newspapers will send you their flyers. After you file with the county clerk's office, you must publish the notice in a newspaper.

4. Go online. Some county's have online forms for you to fill out. Most county's have PDF versions of the forms for you to mail back. Then newspapers (some you have never heard of) will send you their flyers. After you file with the county clerk's office, you must publish the notice in a newspaper.

   www.LegalZoom.com is a popular Web site that many people use for obtaining all of the legal forms you'll need in your business.

   If you do an Internet search for filing a DBA, be careful. You will get Web sites that charge a lot and scare you by telling you all the things that you have to do. Use these words to search: fictitious business name (FBN) and your county name/state [Fictitious Business Name McLeod County]. Look for Web sites that seem like they belong to the county, the county clerk/recorder or the state. Not a legal firm or company.

Publishing

Within 30 days after filing a DBA, a copy of the statement must be published in a newspaper of general circulation in the county in which the principal place of business is located. The notice must appear once per week for four successive weeks with at least five days between the notices.

An affidavit of the published filing must be sent to the County Clerk within 30 days after the publication.

If your county has no publication, then the county of the state capital usually is where you must publish the notice.

Re-Filing

A fictitious name statement expires five years from the date it was filed. If there have been no changes (the individuals are the same) the re-filing fee is less than the original filing or there may be no additional fee if filed within 40 days. After 40 days, you will need to file again.

If there has been any change in the residence address of a registered owner, you need to notify the Clerk.

It is your responsibility to re-file before the five years expires. However, we have noticed that newspapers whose primary purpose is filing DBA's will notify you.

Because we give seminars primarily in Arizona, California, and Nevada, we are going to outline the DBA process in those states. Your local SBA (www.SBA.gov) is a good place for these types of answers.

Arizona
Arizona does not require that you have a DBA. However if you would like to, you can do so with the Secretary of State (www.AZSoS.gov) for $10.

California
Alameda County
Alameda County Clerk-Recorder's Office, 1106 Madison Street, Oakland, CA 94607. The fee is $29 for the first business name and $7 for each additional business name. You can research Fictitious Business Names online at no charge. www.acgov.org/index.htm.

Fresno County
Go to www.Co.fresno.ca.us or call 559-488-3246. The fee is $35 for the first business name and $7 for each additional business name.

Kern County
County Clerk of Kern County, 1115 Truxtun Avenue, Bakersfield, CA 93301 661-868-3588. www.co.kern.ca.us/ctyclerk/dba/default.asp. The fee is $30 for the first business name and $6 for each additional business name.

Los Angeles County
The cheapest for Los Angeles County is Paramount Journal (800-540-1870) who will publish your DBA for $58 + $23 ($81) to the country clerk. Or go to www.lavote.net/CLERK/Business_Name.cfm. The fee is $23 for the first business name and $4 for each additional business name.

Monterey County
Monterey County Clerk, PO Box 29, Salinas, CA 93902, 831-755-5450 to speak with a staff member. www.co.monterey.ca.us/Recorder/ficbusnm.htm. The fee is $30 for the first business name and $7 for each additional business name.

Napa County
Napa County Recorder/Clerk PO Box 298, Napa CA 94559-0298, clerk@co.napa.ca.us, www.co.napa.ca.us/GOV/Departments/DeptPage.asp?DID=28000&LID=622 707-253-4247 The fee is $30 for the first business name and $6 for each additional business name.

Orange County
Orange County, go to www.ocrecorder.com/FBNFiling.asp. The fee is $27 for the first business name. The Web site has a list of newspapers where you can file. The cheapest we have found is $20 with a coupon at 949-589-9990. –

Riverside County
Fictitious Business Name Statement (ACR 500) E-Form. PO Box 751, Riverside CA 92502-0751 or 82-675 Hwy 111 Room 113, Indio CA 92201 951-486-7000. http://riverside.asrclkrec.com The fee is $35 for the first business name and $7 for each additional business name.

Sacramento County
Business License Unit of the Department of Finance, 700 H Street, Room 1710, Sacramento, CA 95814. www.finance.saccounty.net/Tax/FBNGeneral.asp#. The fee is $25 for the first business name and $5 for each additional business name.

San Bernardino County
Auditor/Controller-Recorder, 222 West Hospitality Lane, San Bernardino, CA 92415-0022 909-386-8970 www.co.san-bernardino.ca.us/acr/RecSearch.htm. The fee is $40 for the first business name and $10 for each additional business name.

San Diego County
San Diego Recorder/County Clerk, PO Box 121750, San Diego, CA 92112-1750 http://arcc.co.san-diego.ca.us/arcc/services/fbn_info.aspx Attn: FBN. The fee is $30 for the first business name and $5 for each additional business name.

San Mateo County
www.smcare.org/clerk/fictitious The fee is $34 for the first business name and $5 for each additional business name.

Santa Barbara County
www.sbcvote.com/ClerkRecorder/FictitiousBusinessName.aspx#text The fee is $33 for the first business name and $6 for each additional business name.

Solano County
County Clerk, 675 Texas St, Ste 1900, Fairfield CA 94533-6337 707-784-7510. The fee is $24 for the first business name and $5 for each additional business name.

Sonoma County
Sonoma County Clerk, 2300 County Center Drive, Ste. B-177, Santa Rosa, CA 95403 707-565-3700 or 707-565-3800. The fee is $34 for the first business name and $7 for each additional business name.

Stanislaus County
County Clerk, PO Box 1670, 1021 I St Ste 101, Modesto CA 95353 209-525-5250. The fee is $34 for the first business name and $7 for each additional business name.

Ventura County
For Ventura County, go to http://recorder.countyofventura.org/clerk.htm. The fee is $53. The fee is $53 for the first business name and $10 for each additional business name.

Yuba County
County Recorder, 915 8th St Ste 107, Marysville, CA 95901. The fee is $30 for the first business name and $5 for each additional business name.

Nevada

Clark County
A Fictitious FIRM Name DBA is required for all businesses that plan to use a name different than their legal or corporate name. County Clerk, Attn: FFN, PO Box 551604, Las Vegas, NV 89155-1604. You can file online using www.NevadaTax.nv.gov/web. The fee is $20 and the renewal is $20.

Employer Identification Number (EIN)

If your business is a sole proprietor with employees or independent contractors, you will need to obtain an Employer Identification Number (EIN). Customers will use this number to report payments they make to you. While sole proprietors without employees can use their Social Security numbers for tax reporting purposes, some find it beneficial to have an EIN when opening a bank account or applying for a resale certificate. Contact your local IRS office to obtain an EIN or call the IRS at 800-829-1040.

We have an EIN and whenever we are doing business, we use the EIN. For instance, if we were to go into a bank for a business loan, the name on the loan would be Rounds, Miller and Associates. Instead of using our personal Social Security Number, we would use the EIN. It is the business we are representing, rather than us.

If you do have employees, check out the payroll services. We have heard that for as little as $15 per payroll period they will prepare your payroll. Although payroll is not difficult, there are taxes and deadlines that must be adhered to.

Taxpayer Identification Numbers (TIN)

Many times people become confused because the terms, words or acronyms can mean the same thing or different things. Here are some of the most commonly used phrases for your business number. The TIN is the unique identification number that IRS uses for you. The TIN can be:

SSN   Social Security Number
EIN   Employer Identification Number
ITIN Individual Taxpayer Identification Number
ATIN Taxpayer Identification Number for Pending US Adoptions
PTIN Preparer Taxpayer Identification Number (your accountant's number)

PARTNERSHIP

Going into business with another individual other than your spouse is a partnership. Although partnerships are easy to start, consider a formal partnership agreement. In a partnership, the other person can create liabilities (put you in debt) and has access to assets—with or without your knowledge or consent.

Partnerships are good when one individual has skills or resources that the other doesn't (opposites attract) or the two of you have a commonality (values, vision and skills) that encourages you to join forces. On the other hand, in a partnership there are often feelings of an inequitable situation. One partner is doing more work, contributing more money, taking out more money than the other partner. This is why you want a partnership agreement.

When creating a partnership, what the partners are contributing can be money, time or resources. One way to be equitable in a partnership, is when one partner wants to take money out, the other partner(s) get an equal amount. So if someone is requesting $10, the cost to the business is $20.

Contact us about Pre-Paid Legal Services. Pre-Paid Legal Services services for the home-based such as contract review, collections, access to an attorney, IRS issues. Contact Or go to your local library and reference Nolo Press's (www.Nolo.com) book *Form a Partnership*. Many office supply stores carry Nolo Press books and generic legal forms. Many people have commented that they have used www.LegalZoom.com. Our local library's Web site has usable legal forms for free.

A partnership files an IRS Form 1065. The partnership profit or loss is reported on IRS Form K1, and the profit's tax or business loss is reported onto each partner's individual 1040 income tax return.

You are called a **partner owner** in a partnership.

CORPORATION

A corporation is an incorporated business that is owned by an individual or individuals. It is like giving birth because once you form a corporation; it has a life separate from you.

Guidelines whether to create a corporation are:

1. You (or your spouse) have assets to protect.

2. The type of business you're going into is prone to lawsuits. The advantage of a corporation is that a **corporation stands alone** (corporate veil). This means that if you are sued, it's the corporation that gets sued. Your personal assets are still protected.

3. You're planning to sell or go public with the business.

4. You're planning to have employees.

Disadvantages of creating a corporation for a one-person business:

1. If you want a salary, the corporation pays you a salary. At the end of the year, you pay income tax on your salary. So the same money is taxed twice—once through the corporation taxes and once through your personal income taxes.

2. The minimum state tax that a corporation pays is around $800. Even if the corporation doesn't do any business this year, you would still need to pay the $800.

3. The corporation has to be acting like a corporation—you must follow the rules (issuing stocks, and corporate minutes).

The Secretary of State is where you incorporate in your state. Contact this office for specifics.

You are called an **officer** of a corporation.

There are different types of corporations. They include a C Corp, a Subchapter S Corporation, an LLC, a nonprofit corporation and foreign corporation.

C Corp

A C Corporation is a closed or closely held corporation. This is a common type of corporation for the small business.

The stock is issued to the people running the company or people you know. Nancy remembers growing up that her dad had half the stock in the Miller Ranch Corporation and her mom had half the stock in the corporation. Nobody could buy stock from mom or dad. New stock was never issued. When Mike was incorporated, he held 100 percent of the stock.

How the C Corporation differs from a business you hear about on Wall Street is that they are publicly traded. During the dot com era, there was much excitement about going public. What a corporation wanted to do was to become successful enough to take it public.

The first step to taking a company public was that it had to be successful. And that was with a capital SUCCESSFUL. The idea was that the company was growing so much that the business needed more money A LOT MORE MONEY. So the stock becomes public and people that didn't know who the people were would be able to invest money in the business.

The second step was to have all the accounting in order. As a mom and pop operation if you called a pencil an asset one time and another time called it office supplies, it didn't matter. However, when a business goes public there are more rules and conformity to follow.

The exciting part of going public is for the employees. Usually when people are hired, employees are given stock and during their employment may get or buy more stock shares. Until the company goes public, the stock is kinda like a nice piece of paper with a lot of potential. You can't take potential to the bank. When the company goes public the price of the shares goes up. Then, from potential to cashing in becomes exciting.

There are a few things that you must do to behave like a corporation. In no particular order they are:

Articles of Incorporation: When you form the corporation, the Secretary of State will want a copy of your Articles of Incorporation. When you go and open your business banking, the bank will want a copy of the Articles of Incorporation. There are examples of Articles of Incorporation on the Internet. You do not need a lawyer to do this unless you are uncomfortable with the process. The Articles are like the structure of a house—they don't change much. You might remodel but not frequently.

Bylaws: Are the operating rules of the corporation. These can be changed like changing the interior of the house. You can even change it back to the old way. Bylaws are the written record of your rules.

Annual meeting: Once a year you have a meeting and a record is kept of this meeting. Have you even belonged to an organization and they would announce the annual membership meeting or something similar? Yep, that's what they were doing—the legal stuff.

You may be asking, "But it's only me, how do I have a meeting with myself?" Ever heard of talking to yourself or sitting down to brainstorm? The annual meeting doesn't have to be formal; it just needs to be recorded as the Annual Meeting Minutes. Nancy remembers when her mother learned that they were supposed to have an annual meeting. Many nights after supper dishes were done, her mom would sit down at the desk and construct the minutes to the meeting. Don't do that!

Issuing stock: Remember our little story about going public and the stock, well, you have to issue the stock. It's easy these days. Go to the office supply stores (or online) and purchase the stationery supplies for issuing stock.

There are services that will charge you a yearly fee for the boilerplate records. If you want to pay their fee, go ahead. It's not necessary; you can easily do it yourself.

Here is a little tip, remember that you are a corporate officer. Sign your documents as president. Establish the difference between you the individual and you the corporation.

Subchapter S Corporation

An individual, a partnership, or a corporation can create a Sub S corporation. Although a Sub S is a corporation, the double taxation of the C Corporation is eliminated with the pass through of the money. Pass through entities report the income and losses of the business on the individual tax returns. Check with your accountant/CPA when deciding which entity would be best for you.

LLC (Limited Liability Company)

This business type has become popular during the past decade. An LLC can be formed by an individual or by partners. The advantage of an LLC is that it does not have the double taxation that an individual who has formed a corporation has. The disadvantage is that the protection from liability is not as strong as the corporate veil. It is possible that in the future the LLC may not be as popular as they once were.

Each state has their own rules, regulations and procedures for LLC. You are called a member in a LLC and you create Articles of Organization. The IRS does not consider an LLC a business structure.

Nonprofit Corporation

In this organization, no stockholder or trustee shares in profits or losses. A nonprofit usually exists to accomplish some charitable, humanitarian, or educational purpose. Some examples are hospitals, colleges and universities, and foundations. Such groups are exempt from corporate income taxes (except for Unrelated Business Income), and donations to these groups may be tax deductible for the donor. A nonprofit corporation can accept private or public grant money and apply for tax-exempt status with the IRS.

When a publicly traded corporation needs money, they issue more stock. When a nonprofit corporation needs money, they hold a fundraiser. Nonprofit corporation status means the corporation was not organized for the purpose of earning a profit, and that it qualifies under section 501(c) (3). However, a nonprofit corporation can pay its officers. Some nonprofits pay their officers very well!

Foreign Corporations (Nevada or Delaware)

Corporations are formed at the state level. Each state has different rules about their corporations. When you form a corporation in a state other than the one in which you live, it's called a foreign corporation.

If you have gone to real estate seminars, they may have encouraged you to form a foreign corporation in order to better protect your assets. Some of the advantages of a foreign corporation are taxes. In Nevada there are no corporate income taxes, no capital stock tax, no stock transfer fee or tax, no tax on corporation shares, to name a few. Another reason why businesses incorporate in another state is the increased privacy protection of stock holders.

Although the foreign corporations do have their advantages, as a small business without many assets, this game requires a lot of additional paperwork and may cost more than it saves.

We went to a tax day sponsored by several state organizations (IRS, Franchise Tax Board, Board of Equalization, and INS); one speaker addressed this issue very frankly. He said one way or another; the state will get its taxes.

Nevada has no franchise tax; no corporate income tax; no personal income tax; no capital stock tax; no stock transfer fee or tax; no tax on corporation shares; and no succession tax.

Diversity Owned Business

There might come a time when being a ethnic minority-, women-, veteran-, service-, disabled-business will provide you with an advantage. Few consumers care if you are either a diversity-owned business, although we have known women who make an effort to first look for women-owned business or smaller businesses before going to the big guys.

Having a diversity designation helps when you are bidding on government contracts or working with casinos. It only tips the scales in your direction slightly. You have to be as good as the competition. For the casino, being able to document that they use diversity businesses can make a big difference for them and their business practices.

Information and details are available through your city's mayor or state's governor office, and agencies such as the department of transportation.

You may want to consider joining the National Association of Women Business Owners (NAWBO) 800-556-2926 www.NAWBO.org.

BUSINESS ADDRESSES

Depending upon your situation and your circumstances, there are several options for your business address.

Home Address
Instead of spending your money on office space, your home can also function as your business office. You may want to create the image that you are operating as a business—not a hobby. Put Suite 301 on your house or change Apartment 101 to Suite 101. If you live within a homeowners association, it may have restrictions. Check your CC&R (covenants, conditions, and restrictions) for clarification.

Office or Professional Suites
These suites are small offices rented by the month, day, or hour. Suites are a nice way to have people stop by your office without inviting them to your home. They provide conference rooms and a receptionist to greet customers and answer the telephone. In addition, they often offer a full range of secretarial services.

Post Office Box
A popular choice for start-up, home-based, mail order and Internet businesses is renting a Post Office box. The Post Office rental for a box is about $48/$76/$136 per year (small/medium/large). Check the rates in your area.

Private Mailboxes (PMB)
An alternative to a Post Office box is a private mailbox. The most popular of these franchises is The UPS Store (formerly Mail Boxes, Etc.). Usually these addresses begin with the street address, followed by the unit—904 Silver Spur Road, #807 PMB 103. The box is only 3"x5"x15". These suites rent for $15/$20/$25 per month. Check the rates in your area.

Because private mailboxes are not authorized substations of the USPS, they cannot use the words *Post Office*. Suite 807, Box 332, Penthouse Suite, or 2nd Floor could all be used. Contact the owner of the private mailbox and work out the desired wording.

What type of business structure you want to be is entirely up to you. They all have their pros and cons. Asking people what you should do may not be your best course. Think about what you want the business to be. If it is just a hobby type, then a sole proprietorship is just fine. To get the best use of your money, a sole proprietorship and taking as many home office expenses as possible would be a good way to go. If you want to protect yourself and your money, then a corporation may be the direction to take. If you don't want to do this alone, consider a partnership. The decision is yours.

CHAPTER 7 LEGAL THINGS

There are other things that you need to deal with as a business. They're not difficult but at times are confusing. The city or state may require a business license. If you're dealing with food, it's the health department. Then there's sales tax for the state. Guarantees, warranties and other stuff will be uncomplicated here.

CITY BUSINESS LICENSE

If your business is going to operate within the law, it may be necessary to obtain a license or permit in the city or county in which you will be doing business. If the business is a service and performs any portion of its work in cities outside its operational center, you may be required to obtain licenses in those cities as well. For a start-up, home-based, mail order or Internet business, the location of your office may determine your city for a city license, not where your customers are located. Different cities have different requirements for the business license.

There have been some interesting stories about cities enforcing the business license. One city's employees would go to weddings and when the photographer took the first picture inquired to the photographer whether they had a city business license.

A student shared that he was unloading into the client's living room from his truck which was parked in the driveway of the client's home. As he turned around, there was a police officer asking about the city's business license.

Another city requires that you have to park the car in the garage (you can't change the garage into a recording studio and then park the car on the street). Several cities require that you notify the neighbors. Some cities have the fire inspector look over the business.

Different types of businesses may be subject to special restrictions (or zoning). For instance, a mail order business may be allowed in the home while a direct-sales operation may not. Repair services may be allowed only if they don't involve the use of toxic chemicals. Food services may be disallowed. The city may allow the home as an administrative office for the business.

Home-based businesses are not permitted to change the appearance of the neighborhood. A home-based business may be prohibited from using advertising or equipment that can be viewed from the street. Some cities restrict all home-based business operation.

Business licenses provide the city with a source of **revenue** and a means of controlling the types of businesses that operate within their jurisdictions. The way the cities computes that license is different. Our city has a base and then a couple of dollars for every $_____ over that. Other cities are based on the number of employees.

City business licenses are renewable yearly (January-December) or annually from when you first applied for the license. The cost is around $100+ per year.

The application will consist of such specifics as name, business address, type of business, number of employees, expected gross, vehicles to be operated, and any other information that may be relevant.

In **Nevada** a business license (state business license) is needed for each person, corporation, partnership, business association and any other similar organization that conducts an activity for profit. Obtain the license from the Department of Taxation. Business License Office: 500 S Grand Central Pkwy, Las Vegas, NV 89101 702-455-4252. The local SBA may be able to assist you with the business license.

In the City of Los Angeles, a Business Tax Registration Certificate (TRC) is the original copy of your Business License and is about $99 a year. A small business with $100,000 or less of taxable and nontaxable gross receipts may qualify for a Small Business Exemption.

In Riverside the business license fees are currently $45 for initial licensing and $30 for annual renewal for unincorporated areas of Riverside County. Fee exemptions are granted for various agricultural activities, certain residential businesses, places of worship, and specific nonprofit organizations.

Nearly all cities require a city business license. Call your local city hall and ask for the city license desk. Ask what the **guidelines** are for a start-up, home-based, mail order or Internet business.

OTHER PERMITS

If your business involves making food, you will need to obtain a health department permit and be compliant with food-handling requirements. The use of your own kitchen may not be legal. Check into the rental of facilities already in compliance. The rental fee is usually small. Check out caterers, churches, community halls, company cafeterias, cooking schools, Elk lodges, industrial kitchens, Lions lodges, Masonic temples, Moose lodges, resorts, restaurants, Rotary halls, summer camps, and university cafeterias as possible health department approved facilities.

There are a lot of catering companies in the New York City area that have popped up. To keep expenses down, new caterers use their kitchen to prepare the food. The food's great. However, in New York to be legal, catering companies must use a health department approved kitchen. So, New Yorkers have an acronym TBI—tasty but illegal.

Other inquires that you could make would be about zoning, building safety, and hazardous material.

Additional permits could be a license for a circus or carnival, peddlers permit; public dance hall, taxicab, scrap metal dealer, license to sell fire arms, message establishments, bingo license and secondhand dealer license. If you are having a garage sale, check if your city requires a permit.

A Home Occupation Permit is required in the State of **Nevada** and may be obtained from the local government office.

Car Sign

If you would like to use your automobile to advertise your business, check with your local city hall for guidelines. One city we checked with allowed home-based businesses to advertise on one vehicle only.

If you live in a homeowners association, a vehicle with signage may be considered a *commercial vehicle*. The homeowners association may have regulations for commercial vehicles—such as parking outside the complex rather than on the street or in guest parking.

If you have a sign on your car, you may be considered a commercial vehicle and subject to a commercial vehicle registration.

Recently Nancy had a situation where a car sign would have made her client unhappy. Nancy went to the home of a client to help him organize and de-clutter his home, and he had a panic attack when he saw her car in his driveway. What if the car had a huge neon sign on it saying **CLUTTEROLOGIST**? What would the neighbor's think!

If you want to use your auto as a business expense, the information is covered in Chapter 8.

SALES TAX PERMIT

These may be called a resale number, a wholesale number or a tax exempt number, and all of these deal with the sales tax. In the State of California this is called the **Seller's Permit**.

If you are providing a service, installation or repairs, you do not have to have a sales tax permit.

If you fabricate or assemble the product, you add sales tax and you would need a sales tax permit. You have made the product more valuable by putting it together.

Anyone who purchases items for resale or who provides a taxable service must obtain a seller's permit number.

You can easily apply for a permit by calling the State Board of Equalization, going to their office, or using their Web site.

Many states have temporary seller's permits. For instance, if you sell Christmas trees, your business isn't for the full year, just November and December. If you are exhibiting at a trade show, conference, or convention, talk to the coordinator as they may issue you a run-of-the-show seller's permit.

Reporting

The state requires the filing of a report **annually** or **quarterly**. When the state asks for the sales tax money, they are not taking money away from you. You have been able to hold the money for three to twelve months.

The state will send this report form. Your accountant can complete it if you would like. Failure to properly report sales tax collected may result in the loss of the resale privilege as well as more serious penalties. The following information will be asked on the sales tax report:

1. Gross sales.

2. Purchase price of product purchased without sales tax and used for purposes other than resale.

3. Sales to other retailers for purposes of resale (dealers, wholesalers, resellers).

4. Non-taxable labor (repair and installation).

5. Sales to the United States government.

6. Sales in interstate or foreign commerce to out-of-state consumers. (Only your state customers pay sales tax—that is why it is called **State Sales Tax**.)

7. Other exempt transactions.

Additional Variables

So, how do you let the customer know about sales tax? There are three ways that you can list (identify) sales tax for your customer:

1. Post a sign stating that sales tax will be added (like at McDonalds).

2. List a separate amount for sales tax ($19.95 plus $1.40 sales tax).

3. Specifically include sales tax ($30 including sales tax), like prices listed at a swap meet or street fair.

What rate do you charge for customers in other states? You only charge customer's in your state, because that's where your business is. Have you seen an ad, like Lillian Vernon states: shipments to NV, NY State, SC, TN, VA and VT, apply the applicable sales tax. They are collecting sales tax in those states because they have a base of operation in those states. There is no such thing as a multiple-state sale tax. A company such as Starbucks would collect sales tax in all 50 states because they have stores in all 50 states.

There is currently no Internet tax where purchases on the Internet are taxed. If you do make a purchase on the Internet and the business' physical presences is in your state, then the business would charge the appropriate **state** sales tax rate.

As of this time, the State of New York has created what is called an Amazon tax which could be tax/sales tax for online purchases. With the change in the economy, everyone is looking for a new source of income. Time will tell if an Amazon tax happens or not.

If you don't have a seller's permit and a customer pays you sales tax, you must turn the sales tax over to the state (or return in back to the customer). If the customer overpays you sales tax, you must either return the excess to the customer or turn the excess over to the state.

Shipping ~~and Handling~~

Take the phrase shipping and handling out of your vocabulary. You might think that setup costs, rush charges, the time it takes you to pack up the order, the cost of the shipping material, the box, the tape all justify the *handling* cost. These are a part of your overhead. In California, the State Board of Equalization is starting to look into companies that charge S&H fee.

While shipping (postage) is an actual cost, many people have tried to make up their profit by charging a great deal for S&H. Many people don't declare the profit on this line on their business income.

If you have any questions, call the state and they will be happy to help you before a major problem occurs. If you have taken their tax seminar class previously.

Because we give seminars primarily in Arizona, California, and Nevada, we are going to outline the Sales tax in those states. Your local SBA (www.SBA.gov) is a good place for these types of answers.

Arizona

Arizona states that casual sales between individuals are not subject to sales tax. www.AZDOR.gov and www.AZtaxes.gov.

Nevada

Nevada Department of Taxation the Combined Sales and Use Tax Return. You do not charge sales tax to entities where you have received a resale certificate, Federal Government, State of Nevada, school districts religious or charitable organization are not taxed either.

California

A seller's permit is obtained through the **State Board of Equalization** in California. This number usually begins with **SR**. California is in the process of going to an electronic filing format. www.BOE.CA.gov.

Resale Certificate

The sales tax permit is used for purchasing those items that will be resold to your customers without charging you sales tax. Not everything you buy will be tax exempt. Only those items the customer buys from you are tax exempt. Once a resale tax number has been issued, it's imperative that you use it only for the purpose for which it was intended (purchasing taxable items for resale).

The penalties for misuse are serious and may involve a heavy fine and/or a jail sentence. The rule of thumb is: if there is no intention to resell the purchase through the business, do not use the resale number.

For example, you might go to an office supply store to buy a ream of paper. If you use that ream of paper in your printer to print a book, then the end user will be your

---

BOE-230 (7-02)

GENERAL RESALE CERTIFICATE

STATE OF CALIFORNIA
BOARD OF EQUALIZATION

California Resale Certificate

I HEREBY CERTIFY:

1. I hold valid seller's permit number: _____

2. I am engaged in the business of selling the following type of tangible personal property:

_____

3. This certificate is for the purchase from _____ of the item(s) I have listed in paragraph 5 below.   [Vendor's name]

4. I will resell the item(s) listed in paragraph 5, which I am purchasing under this resale certificate in the form of tangible personal property in the regular course of my business operations, and I will do so prior to making any use of the item(s) other than demonstration and display while holding the item(s) for sale in the regular course of my business. I understand that if I use the item(s) purchased under this certificate in any manner other than as just described, I will owe use tax based on each item's purchase price or as otherwise provided by law.

5. Description of property to be purchased for resale:

6. I have read and understand the following:

For Your Information: A person may be guilty of a misdemeanor under Revenue and Taxation Code section 6094.5 if the purchaser knows at the time of purchase that he or she will not resell the purchased item prior to any use (other than retention, demonstration, or display while holding it for resale) and he or she furnishes a resale certificate to avoid payment to the seller of an amount as tax. Additionally, a person misusing a resale certificate for personal gain or to evade the payment of tax is liable, for each purchase, for the tax that would have been due, plus a penalty of 10 percent of the tax or $500, whichever is more.

NAME OF PURCHASER

SIGNATURE OF PURCHASER, PURCHASER'S EMPLOYEE OR AUTHORIZED REPRESENTATIVE

PRINTED NAME OF PERSON SIGNING   TITLE

ADDRESS OF PURCHASER

TELEPHONE NUMBER   DATE
(   )

---

customer and you are sales tax exempt. If you use that ream of paper to create a flyer, you are the end user and you pay the sales tax.

Now that you have your sales tax permit, when you go to a store to purchase goods that will be resold to your customer, fill out the resale certificate (or something similar) so that you will not be charged sales tax on those items. Likewise, if a customer of yours wants to sell your product to their customers, have your customer fill out this form and you hang onto it so that if you are audited by the State, you can prove that your customer was buying from you to resell it.

Having the sales tax permit doesn't allow you to not pay sales tax anymore. The sales tax permit is only for those items that you will be selling to your customers.

TRADEMARK

Because of the amount of advertising, promotion, publicity, and the subsequent reputation that is connected with goods and services, trademarks tend to become the identity under which people recognize and purchase a particular line of goods or services.

You will need to provide the US Patent and Trademark Office (www.USPTO.gov) with five samples of the mark as it is used. A supply of samples of the mark, logo, package, and letterhead will suffice.

The ™ (trademark) may be placed on any logo, name, slogan, etc. as fair warning to others in the trade that you are using this as your trademark.

The ™ (service mark) is usually placed on a logo or other device for firms that are dealing with a service rather than a product. The rights, restrictions, and cautions are the same as when using the ™.

The ® (registered mark) is allowed on a mark only after the mark has been officially approved and granted by the US Patent and Trademark Office.

As a result, the trademark may become as valuable as, or even more valuable than, the goods or services it represents. A trademark:

1. Is a word, symbol, slogan, or even a distinctive sound that identifies and distinguishes the goods and services of one party from those of another?

2. Takes 6-13 months to be granted, depending on the category selected and the backlog of work. There are 34 classes of goods and 8 classes of services that can be trademarked. It's possible to register the same name in different classes of goods or services.

3. Is granted for a period of 10 years and is renewable, as long as the mark is maintained in an active status.

4. Costs $375 (electronic filing) per submission, not including charges for the artwork and forms.

5. Has a maintenance fee of about $350.

If either the name or the graphic portion of the trademark is deceptively similar to another trademark in the same category, the US Patent and Trademark Office may deny the registration due to its similarity.

A preliminary search can be run by a patent agent, patent attorney, or the US Patent and Trademark Room of a patent library to determine if the mark is available or taken. Many of the libraries offer the Trademark Search service for a minimal fee. The Pasadena City Library (626-405-4052) is one example.

If you are interested in more information on this topic, you may want to purchase Trademarks and Copyrights for the Clueless®. Details are available in the back of this book.

WARRANTIES

Warranties and exchanges are a matter of policy rather than of the law. The law states that you must live up to the representations that you make. Warranties are typically the manufacturer's responsibility. You might like to extend the warranty to establish yourself as better than your competition.

When Rounds, Miller and Associates was a partner in a computer company that sold network systems to law firms, we extended the manufacturer's warranty from 90 days to 1-year for very specific reasons.

1. We knew the manufacturer. They had a consistency in their quality control.

2. We knew the computer industry. If the part did not break within that first 90 days, the likelihood that it would break in the next year was small.

3. If someone was buying our product on price alone, after a year they were unlikely to remember who or where they bought it.

4. If a customer had a part break, we would replace it. We had profited from them throughout the year and the hard cost of the part was pennies. It was great customer service.

GUARANTEES

A guarantee is whatever you decide that it is, it is your store's policy. The government doesn't say what a guarantee needs to be. On the other hand, you can use the guarantee to increase your success.

Here is a ground rule for a start-up, home-based, mail order and Internet business: offer a 100 percent, no hassle, no questions, unconditional money-back guarantee.

First, if you are using a Post Office box or they have not heard of you before, by offering a money-back guarantee, you are giving them some assurance that they have recourse if something goes wrong. Second, people believe what they see, and obviously this must be a quality product—no one gives that kind of guarantee on junk.

Third, the return rate from people sending back merchandise is low. How much stuff do you have right now which, based on the guarantee, you are entitled to send back? We just do not bother to do it.

How many of us, when reconciling our checking accounts, will call the bank when we discover a difference of $1? $5? $10? $20? We all have a different tolerance (or AQ—aggravation quotient) level. For some of us, our time is worth more than the hassle of one dollar.

Your customers are the same! It would not be worth the time, hassle, and effort to return the product. Of the customers that have a problem, only 30 percent of them will voice their complaint.

Another reason to offer an unlimited money-back guarantee is to extend the time of the guarantee in the customer's mind. As a start-up, home-based, mail order and Internet business, by extending the date you give people the opportunity to forget. If by contrast you offer a 30-day money-back guarantee, then by day 21 your customers will be thinking, "Should I send it back? Shouldn't I? Should I? Shouldn't I?" Within the 30 days, they will most likely send it back. Why? Not because they don't not like it, but because you have limited the time they have to make up their minds.

Can you remember where you were 60 days ago? 90 days ago? Unless the purchase was linked to a specific date (such as a holiday or personal event), 60 days ago seems like a year.

RETURNS

Returns are a part of a normal business. According to the National Retail Federation, the return rate was 8.7 percent of sales in 2007. If your return rate is higher than that, adjust your business model as something may be wrong. If your return rate is lower than that, you're doing better than national average.

If a customer returns a product, see if you can find the trend for your own product and market knowledge. If, for example, the customer sends back the product and states that it was broken in transit, change packing materials.

If the customer returns the product and states that it broke when little Johnny played with it for ten minutes, you might have a quality control problem. Go back to the manufacturer. Or state: not intended for children under the age of 55.

If the customer returns the product and states that he or she expected it to be bigger, you need to check your advertising. Put some qualifications on size or expectations. You may have too much hype in your advertising.

Here is how we look at returns:

- If one person returns a product, we consider it an accident. That one person had a bad experience with the product.

- If two people return a product, we consider that a coincidence. Coincidences don't happen that often, so we begin to take a closer look at how we can stop it from happening again.

- If three or more people return a product with similar reasons, we have developed a habit—an unpleasant habit—and now it's time to make changes!

DELIVERY

> ### 50 recipes from the chili cook-off $30; 4-6 weeks for delivery

Mail order sales are governed by rules of the Federal Trade Commission (FTC) and various state laws. In general, these guidelines are:

The customer's order must be shipped within 30 days or one calendar month, whichever is greater, unless otherwise stated.

If it appears that the customer's order will not be shipped on time, you must notify the customer in writing and in advance, giving a definite new date. You must offer the customer the opportunity to either cancel the order with a refund or consent to a delayed shipping date.

Your notice must contain a self-addressed stamped card or envelope with which the customer can indicate a preference. If the customer does not respond to this notice, you may assume the customer agrees to the delay. Even if the customer has consented to an indefinite delay, the customer retains the right to cancel the order at any time before the item has been shipped.

If the customer chooses to cancel an order that has been paid for by check or money order, you must mail the customer a refund within seven business days. If the customer cancels an order for which he or she paid by credit card, you must credit the customer's account within one billing cycle following receipt of the customer's request. Store credits or vouchers in place of a refund are not acceptable on delayed deliveries.

In the event that the item the customer ordered is unavailable, you may not send the customer substitute merchandise without the customer's express consent.

Advertising is the representation you make to the customer. It is a form of contractual law, a contract between you and the customer, the recipient of goods. If you do not live up to that representation, you are in breach of contract.

Example: if a customer sends you $30 and you send 50 recipes, you have fulfilled your contract. If you sent only 49 recipes, you would be in breach. The customer has three choices:

1. They can demand their money back, incurring no penalty.

2. They can demand that you complete the order at no cost to them.

3. They can allow you to substitute something of equal or comparable value.

Good customer service will prevent many problems, and you will probably be in legal compliance.

INSURANCE

Insurance comes in many forms and sizes. Sometimes it is appropriate for a start-up, home-based, mail order, Internet business and sometimes it is not. To help you better understand what an agent has to offer, here are some easy descriptions of the different types of insurance.

In John T. Reed's book *How to Manage Residential Property for Maximum Cash Flow and Resale Value*, he says, "An insurance policy is **not** a lottery ticket. It's not a way of making money by 'cashing in' when you have a loss." The purpose of insurance is to help you get the business back operational, not to give a handout.

The average premiums and coverages listed here are guidelines and may not be applicable to your situation or state. These figures are based on the following composite: a male, age 38 and in good health, married with children, living in a large metropolitan area, who is a sole proprietor working from home in a service-related business—such as a computer consultant—and who owns $5,000 to $7,000 of business property.

Auto Insurance

Auto insurance covers the loss of business property in the car and the costs of accidents when you or someone on your behalf is driving the car for business purposes. When needed: if you use the car for business purposes other than driving to and from work, especially if you transport equipment or merchandise in the car. Estimated cost of average coverage: $1,600 per year (includes regular accident coverage). If you drive a minimum number of miles, you may be able to be placed in a lower-risk category and pay lower premiums.

As if using your vehicle while conducting your business is covered under your current auto insurance. It may be, it may not be. Have the talk with your agent before anything happens. Be informed.

Homeowners or Renters Insurance

This is one of the most popular forms of personal insurance on the market. The typical homeowner's policy has two main sections: Section I covers your property, and Section II provides personal liability coverage, which covers you in case of lawsuits arising from things that happen on your property. Almost anyone who owns or leases property should have this type of insurance. It is often required by lenders in order to obtain a mortgage.

A standard renter's policy protects your personal property in many cases of theft or damage and may pay for temporary living expenses if your property is damaged so seriously that you can't live in it. It can also protect you from personal liability.

Generally, for a couple hundred dollars a year, you can get renters or homeowners insurance. Check the wording to see if it covers replacement value (the cost of replacing the item new) or current or actual value (the garage sale price).

A rider is an attachment to a policy that modifies its conditions by expanding or restricting benefits or excluding certain conditions from coverage. Start with homeowners or renters insurance and then add the items below as additional riders to the policy. This is usually cheaper than just getting the type of insurance coverage by themselves.

Business-Property Insurance

This protects you from damage or loss to the business property. When needed: if you have any equipment in your home office that is used for business purposes. Estimated cost of average coverage: $50 per year for $5,000 to $7,000 of equipment (as a rider to the homeowner's policy).

Discounts on property insurance rates are sometimes available if you protect your home as follows: fire and smoke alarms, or smoke, heat, or ion detectors approved by Underwriter's Laboratory; dead bolt locks on exterior doors, and home security systems.

To protect your home office from fire and burglary, have the local police and fire departments perform a free inspection. They may recommend additional fire alarms, more secure locks, and perimeter burglar alarms.

Computer Insurance

Computer insurance covers damage to the computer hardware, software, and data. When needed: when computer-related losses are not adequately covered under your property- or small-business insurance policies. Estimated cost of average coverage: $89 per year for $5,000 to $8,000 coverage; $109 per year for $8,000 to $11,000 coverage; $129 per year for $11,000 to $14,000 coverage.

The computer insurance on your homeowner's policy is limited, or you have to pay for a separate rider and there is still a small limit. Check what coverage you actually will have. Many times what you want covered and what you think is covered won't actually be covered.

Computer insurance companies have not been around long. Check out the companies thoroughly. Ask some of your colleagues and find out who they are using.

General Liability Insurance

General liability is primarily concerned with losses caused by negligent acts, bodily injury, property damage on the premises of a business, injury from a product manufactured, or injury occurring in the general operation of a business. When needed: if you do some portion of your work on someone else's premises. Estimated cost of average coverage: included as part of small business insurance; otherwise, about $200 per year.

Liability Insurance

These cover costs of injuries that occur on the property to business-related visitors. When needed: if you ever have delivery people or customers come to your home. Estimated cost of average coverage: $20 per year for $500,000 of coverage (when added as a rider to homeowner's policy).

Malpractice or Errors and Omissions Insurance

These insure against claims or damages that arise out of the services or products you offer. When needed: if your work could inadvertently inflict an injury or loss on the customer—such as tax preparation. Estimated cost of average coverage: comes with small-business insurance; minimum premium approximately $500.

Partnership Insurance

Partnership insurance protects you against suits arising from the actions of any partners in the business. When needed: if you have partners or do joint ventures. Estimated cost of average coverage: a $500 fidelity bond.

Small-Business Insurance

This provides coverage for business losses—including general liability, business interruption, and loss of earnings, errors and omissions, and product liability. These policies can be purchased separately as well. When needed: if you have more extensive inventory or equipment than you can protect by adding a business endorsement or rider to the homeowner's policy. Estimated cost of average coverage: $500 per year.

Workers Compensation Insurance

If you have people working for you (employees), you need to provide them with Workers Compensation Insurance. The cost of this insurance will be based on the business classification and total payroll.

This compensates employees for costs of work-related injuries and also time off the job. When needed: available primarily for employees. If you are incorporated you can get this insurance for yourself. State regulations vary. May be called state disability insurance. Estimate cost of average coverage: bare bones coverage, about $200 per year.

Contact a company called State Fund (www.scif.com) in California for coverage. In **Arizona** contact SCF Arizona at 602-631-2600 or 800-231-4453 www.SCFAZ.com.

In **Nevada**, every business that employs anyone must obtain workers compensation insurance coverage unless that entity is certified by the Commissioner of Insurance as a self-insured employer. Contact the State of Nevada Department of Business and Industry Division of Insurance 702-486-4009 2501 E Sahara Ave Ste 302, Las Vegas NV 89158.

Bonded

Being bonded means that an outside agency (the bonding company) is making a guarantee. For instance, if you were a home cleaning service the bond would mean individuals are not felons and nothing will get stolen.

Grand theft is a crime recognized as a felony by most US States, and involves the deprivation of property. The dollar value could be as low as $400. Check your state for what they consider grand theft.

For more information on bonding, search the Internet for *Getting Bonded for Small Business* and you will find companies that provide this service.

The SBA can be a great source for some of your insurance questions. Call Termquote (800-444-8376) for more information and education. Additional resources: www.4Insurance.com (life, health, auto and home); www.MatrixDirect.com (key person insurance); www.InsureMe.com; www.INSWeb.com (renters, business); www.insure.com; www.einsurance.com; www.insweb.com; www.bestquote.com; and www.quickquote.com.

SUGGESTED ORDER OF EVENTS

Are you overwhelmed with what you have to do and trying to figure out what to do first? Here is our suggestion:

1. First, what will the **name** of your business be? This might imply that you know what you want to sell; however, you can always change the direction of the company once you figure out what people are buying. So at this moment, just a vague idea is good enough.

   Questions to ponder before completing this step: do you want to be a partnership or corporation? Can you get a domain name as close to identical to your business name?

2. File a **DBA**. Getting your fictitious business name will allow you to open a banking account in the business name. If you are using a separate bank account in the business name, then you need a DBA. In this example, we have assumed that you are going to be a sole proprietorship.

   Questions to ponder before completing this step: what is the address of your business (PO Box, PMB or house)?

3. If you plan to sell products, get the **sales tax permit** before you purchase your first inventory or components (raw) parts so that you can show this document to your vendor without paying sales tax.

   Questions to ponder before completing this step: if you are providing labor, you do not need a sales tax permit. If you are buying supplies and having the client reimburse you for those actual expenses (no profit or mark-up) you do not need a sales tax permit. If your yearly volume of products is very low, you don't need a sales tax permit. However, you don't get to make that decision; the State will advise you.

4. **City business license** may be needed when you open a business bank account. This fee could be around $100 a year (each and every year) so having cash flow (also known as customers paying their bills) is useful.

CHAPTER 8 INTERNAL REVENUE SERVICE

This is the exciting part about being a business. There are more business expenses that are deductable when you are a business than when you are an individual. Whether you are a sole proprietorship, partnership or LLC, it's all the same to the IRS (for our discussion here).

If you or your spouse has a full-time job (we'll call you W2'd [Wage and Tax Statement]) when you become a business, you might be able to bring home more money on your W2'd pay check. Here's the scoop.

When you filled out the withholding form for your W4 (Employee's Withholding Allowance Certificate), the number of deduction/withholdings may be small (one or two, for instance). When you create the business, the business will have business expenses (Schedule C on your income taxes). You can change the number of withholdings to a larger number for instance (check with your accountant).

However (and this is the good part) your W2'd pay check is regular income. So these expenses are balanced against the W2'd income. You can wait until next year when you get your refund. Or you can revise your withholdings to a larger number of deductibles. Check with your accountant to determine which would be best in your situation.

OPEN FOR BUSINESS

With a home-based business, you open your doors for business and then buy the things you need. Those expenses (most of them) are a business expense in the current year. Isn't that great! Today I am a business. Tomorrow I create business expenses.

Let's say that we wanted to open a beauty salon. The first thing we would do is find a place to rent, and they would want a deposit, first month and last month's rent. Then you have to buy the equipment: chairs, mirrors and shampoo. The sign outside the building doesn't come for free. The utilities have to be hooked up. And an ad in the newspaper and radio to announce your grand opening are additional expenses. **Now** the doors are open for business.

Every expense that happened before the doors opened for business has to be *amortized* (gradual and periodic reduction of the amount) over a period of time (seven years for instance). So it would be years before you got to enjoy the benefit of those expenses. Let's hope that you're still in business.

Many people ponder the difference between what is a hobby and a business. Here are three factors:

First, in order to take business expenses, you must have a legitimate business. If you create a business just to be able to take advantage of all the home-based business expenses, it is not considered a legitimate business.

Second, prove that you intend to make a profit. A good way to accomplish this is to create a business plan. Attend a seminar given by the Small Business Administration on creating a business plan. There is a difference between intending to make a profit and actually making a profit. There will be times in the life of your business when you have more expenses than income. That's part of business.

Third, work your business on a regular and consistent base. For instance, if you have a multilevel business and are working 40 hours a week for a company, in your calendar enter that for 60 minutes at a time four or five times a week that you are in the office working on the multilevel business.

Document your income and expenses. Just because this may be a part-time business for you doesn't mean you can keep any less documentation than a full-time business.

With a home-based business, your intent is to make a profit and work the business actively and consistently. There are types of businesses that even if there is no profit, won't be considered a hobby. The American auto industry is not a hobby but doesn't often make a profit!

Being a poor business person or not having a business that your family approves of, doesn't make it a hobby.

ACCOUNTING

From the simplest two-column ledger program like Quicken to the completely integrated multitasking, relational accounting programs like Peachtree, accounting software is one of the best reasons to be computerized. Find a program that is appropriate for your needs, style, and business. Talk to your accountant about what software can be imported into his or her system.

If your rule for business is that EVERYTHING goes through the checkbook (you don't pay with cash, you deposit the cash you receive), then having a simple program like Quicken will probably work just fine.

A couple of years ago, Nancy took a class at the local adult school for QuickBooks. What she learned was that some of her questions were not about the software at all. They were accounting questions. So, she took another class on accounting. Basic understanding helps you to be able to ask the questions of your accountant and to use their terms and language. If you are not familiar with accounting procedures, we recommend you take a class or get a good book on the subject.
Here are some common business expenses.

* Mortgage interest or rent

* Gas, electric, water and sewer

* Cleaning crews to dust, vacuum, and empty the trash

- Computers, copiers, fax machines and telephones

- Paper, pens, ink cartridges, postage and postage stamps

- Desks, sofas, coffee tables and other furniture

- Painting, wallpaper, carpeting, and other repairs or remodeling

- Phone bills, cell phones, pagers, and Personal Data Assistants (PDA's)

- Newspapers, magazines, books, and on-line media subscriptions

- Plane fares, hotel, meal, and rental car

- Health, life, dental, vision, disability, and unemployment insurance premiums

- Contributions to Employee Retirement Plans

- Company cars, and even boats

- Advertising

- Bank charges and banking fees

- Charitable contributions

- Credit card fees

- Permits and licenses

- Repairs

- Other expenses that qualifies as *ordinary and necessary* to operate the business

DOCUMENTATION

As a business, you should be keeping two pieces of documentation to backup your business tax expenses.

The first is the cancelled check or bank or credit card statement. Let's say that you go to Office Depot and purchase $100 worth of office supplies. You mutter under your breath, "Why can't the IRS just take my check as the documentation."

That's because the store may ask, "Would you like cash back?" Your eyes light up and you ask for $100.

The second piece of documentation is the receipt, invoice or statements showing exactly what you purchased and for how much. Now your check is $200, of which only $100 is office supplies. Or you buy $50 worth of office supplies and $50 worth of candy. This process is called *itemization* (to list) by the IRS.

If you don't use a check for purchases, a credit card is fine. A credit card has a monthly statement. That statement cannot be altered which is what the IRS is looking for. The NCR copy of your check could be altered as can data in accounting software.

A good policy is to keep documentation for all transactions. Don't assume that if a transaction is under a low dollar figure that the IRS would never ask for it.

One of the most important pieces of documentation is your calendar. Our advice to you is to keep the calendar forever. And the messier (more used) it is, the better.

For instance, let's say the IRS questions a business meal that you had. You pull out your calendar and say "see here it shows that I met Joe at Cheesecake" which was exactly the same thing your receipt indicated.

The IRS doesn't care if you eat at El Cheapo or Chez Expensive for a business expense. A business expense is a business expense. As the business owner, know the difference between cash flow and an IRS expense. With cash flow, you have to have the money in your checkbook to pay for it. So although the IRS doesn't care, the banks don't like you having overdrafts.

Just because you could buy a very expensive car for the business doesn't mean that you should. An expensive car as a business expense doesn't make it cheaper, less expensive or better for you. If you don't have the cash flow to support the car in the first place, taking the business expense in the second place may cause problems.

Intentions

One of the easiest ways to think about whether an expense is a personal or a business expense is to think about the intention of that expense.

For instance if you and another person (not someone working in your business) go out for a meal and you want to pick up the check as a business expense there needs to be a discussion about business. On the receipt, jot a note about what was discussed, who you were with, where the meal was, when it was (the date), and how much was spent.

Do you want to go to Hawaii and call that a business trip? It could be, if done correctly. Before you go to Hawaii, you have to set up business meetings. The meetings should be during the whole time you are there. It doesn't have to be every day and every hour, but it can't be just the first day.

If you have gone to Hawaii and while you were sitting at the beach, you started a conversation with the stranger next to you. He likes you and later becomes your best client. Is that trip a business expense? No. You didn't go to Hawaii with the intention of creating business, it just happened. You didn't set up the meeting on the beach as a business meeting, it just happened.

Sharing

When you start your business, you may want to use what you already own because cash flow is tight.

For those items that you have one of (one car, one computer, or one telephone), then you have to log the use of personal and business.

Car: go to the office supply store and get an auto mileage book. Every time you drive the car, write down the mileage and purpose (personal or business). At the end of the month, add up your business mileage.

Computer: document the usage of the computer for the business. At the end of the month, add it up. This will give you the base price for your Internet service. If you use the computer 20 percent for business, then 20 percent of the provider's bill is a business expense.

Telephone: if you have one phone line, then you must document the business use of that phone. The base charges for the phone are expensed to your personal use. The actual business use is a business expense. When the bills arrive, get out your highlighter and highlight the calls that were business. Add up the cost.

Not Sharing

When you have more than one item or an item that is used exclusively for business and is in the business name, this is how you document the item for your financial records.

Car: if you have two vehicles, decide which one is for business and which one is for personal. All of the expenses for the business vehicle are a business expense.

There are two methods of calculating the expenses of a vehicle. If you don't want to keep all your receipts, you can average the cost by using the government's mileage of 58.5¢ per mile. You may be surprised to know that you are not making money or even breaking even with this method. Most vehicles cost more than 58.5¢ to operate. The advantage is less paperwork.

The other method is actual expense. Keep your gasoline receipts, your insurance costs, your vehicle maintenance and even your vehicle payments.

Computer: If you were to be visited by the IRS and only had one computer, it might be difficult to convince them that you have no personal life and don't use the computer for personal use. Have your kids put games on the computer? The only games that can be on your business computer are those that came with it (like Microsoft solitaire). If there are games, the line to personal usage has been crossed.

Holiday Cards: your holidays cards might be considered a business expense if they promote the business. For instance just signing the holiday cards Mike and Nancy would be considered a personal expense.

On the other hand having the cards pre-printed:

Rounds, Miller and Associates
Mike Rounds and Nancy Miller

could be considered a business expense.

Business Meals

When you go out to eat, keep the receipts. On the receipt document the date, the amount, who you had a meeting with, and what business was discussed. A common misunderstanding is that you don't have to talk the whole time about business. You DO have to talk about business.

If you are a sales person (or making a sales call) also indicate what the percentage of likihood is that this person/company will become a customer/client. What the IRS is looking for, is if you're taking all your cousins out to dinner, one at a time, and calling it a sales call. None of your cousins ever intended to become a client.

Why are business travel meals only a 50 percent business expense? Because the IRS doesn't reward you for eating. You have to eat anyway. The difference between the business travel meal and the business meal is in the documentation. A business travel meal does not need to contain talking about business to be an expense.

A word of advice about locations of meeting for meals. There must be a reasonable expectation of a conversation. A night club, although they may have great food would not necessarily be a reasonable expectation for a conversation with the hundreds of people dancing and talking with the music blaring in the background.

Spouse

Your spouse might enjoy some of the advantages of having a home-based business. For instance, if you have planned a business trip/meeting to a location that your spouse would enjoy, considering bringing your spouse along.

If your spouse is just along for a good time, then the business expenses of the trip are your hotel room (and the spouse stays with you), if you drive to the location your spouse can ride with you for free. Spouse's meals and entertainment are personal expenses.

On the other hand, if your spouse has a bona fide business purpose to be on the trip, then the spouse's expenses become a business expense.

If your spouse is doing something for the business during the trip then the expenses of the trip are a business expense. If a spouse attended the trade show and helped set up the booth, worked the booth during peak times and helped pack everything up, then yes it is a business expense. If your spouse is just tagging along, no. The lodging is paid for you so that part was already covered. Meals are not a business expense.

Home-Office Deduction

To calculate how much of the rent, mortgage interest, and other home expenses can reasonably be deducted, measure the floor space of the home office and divide it by the total area of your house. If your office space comes to 9.5 percent, you can deduct 9.5 percent of the cost of the rent, insurance, mortgage interest, utilities, repairs, and improvements to the property.

The drawback to these prorated deductions is that, since part of the house will be considered business property, the business will be subject to capital gains tax when the house is sold. However, recently the dollar figure has been raised where this is now an almost non-issue.

To qualify to claim expenses for business use of your home, you must meet the following tests.

Your use of the business part of your home must be:

1. Exclusive use. You must use your home business area only for your business. You do not meet the requirements of the exclusive use test if you use the area in question both in business and for personal purposes.

2. Regular. You must use a specific area of your home for business on a continuing basis. For instance 45-60 minutes a day, 4-5 days a week (12 hours a month).

3. For your business. You have no other location where you conduct substantial administrative or management activities of your business.

AND . . . the business part of your home must be **one** of the following

1. Your principal place of business, or

2. You regularly and exclusively use your home office for administrative or management activities for your business and have no other fixed location where you perform such activities, or

3. A place where you meet or deal with customers in the normal course of your business, or

4. You run a day care center at home, or

5. A separate structure (not attached to your home) you use in connection with your business.

Let's take a closer look at exclusive use. That means that your office is your office. Not a place where guests sometimes sleep. Not a place where you store extra clothes in the closet. Look at the bookshelf in the office. What are the titles of the books? Nancy's bookshelf has books like Taming the Paper Tiger, Time Management for Dummies and Side-Tracks Home Executives. Although you may think these are personal books, as a professional organizer, Nancy reads books on organizing and therefore these are business books and are allowable on the bookshelf in the office.

We haven't talked about business entertainment and we're not going to. This is an area that is abused so if you have business entertainment issues, research how to document your activities.

There is a book that is only available through the Internet. *Home Business Tax Savings Made Easy!* that gives tax tips to learn how to keep more of your money.

A great book to answer almost all your questions about what and how to take home-business expenses (as well as other books) is the book *Home Business Tax Deductions* for $34.99. The publisher (**Nolo Press** www.Nolo.com) is a wonderful resource for home-based business. Nolo Press was created by a group of lawyers, and their books deal with a range of legal type issues written in an easy to understand and comprehend fashion.

Two free IRS publications explain the rules for home offices and offer advice on bookkeeping: *Business Use of Your Home #587*, and *Taxpayers Starting a Business #583*. Call 800-829-3676. Deliveries of these publications are within 7-15 working days of request. Or you can go on-line and get a PDF of these publications.

INDEPENDENT CONTRACTORS

As an independent contractor, the payment that you receive is in gross dollars. The client doesn't take out any taxes. You become responsible for taxes, retirement and insurance. Just because you say you're an independent contractor, doesn't always make you an independent contractor.

The determination of whether an individual who performs services for another is performing services in the capacity of an employee, as opposed to services in the capacity of an independent contractor, carries with it significant federal tax consequences.

If you are employed, the employer:

- Must withhold income taxes from the wages paid to employees.

- Must withhold FICA taxes from employees' wages.

- Is required to match the amount of withheld FICA taxes.

- Must pay FICA and FUTA taxes on wages paid to employees, subject to credits for unemployment tax payments made into a state unemployment fund.

As an independent contractor:

- Your payment is not subject to neither income nor Social Security taxes withholdings.

- The client is not required to pay its share of FICA taxes or to pay FUTA taxes.

- You will pay the full amount of your Social Security taxes in the form of self-employment taxes.

- You are generally not entitled to protection from discrimination under either the Civil Rights Act of 1964 or the Age Discrimination in Employment Act of 1986.

- You do not receive rights relating to compensation provided by the Fair Labor Standards Act.

- You are not entitled to certain rights under the Occupational Safety and Health Act of 1970.

Under the common-law test, a worker is an employee if the employer has a right to direct and control when, where, and how the worker performs the tasks. The employer need not exercise control: it is sufficient that the employer has the right to do so.

The Internal Revenue Service has adopted 20 common-law factors to determine whether the requisite control or right to control exists to establish an employer-employee relationship. The IRS has not given any indication as to the weight to be assigned each of the various factors; however, there is an emphasis on the general notion of control.

The 20 factors are the extent to which:

1. The employer instructs the worker on how to complete the task.

2. The employer trains the worker.

3. The employer sets the order or sequence of work completion.

4. The employer pays the worker's business and/or travel expenses.

5. The employer furnishes the worker's tools or materials.

6. The employer has the right to discharge the worker.

7. The worker is integrated into the employer's business.

8. The worker renders his or her services personally.

9. The worker works on the employer's premises.

10. The worker reports orally or in writing.

11. The worker is paid an hourly, weekly, or monthly salary.

12. The worker does not have a significant investment in the tools or machinery.

13. The worker has no potential to realize a significant profit or loss.

14. The worker may **work for others simultaneously**.

15. The worker may hire, fire, supervise, or pay assistance.

16. The worker may make services available to the general public.

17. The worker has the right to terminate the relationship.

18. There is a continuing relationship.

19. There are set hours of work.

20. Full-time work is required.

Since all of these factors may not be pertinent in any given situation, and since all of them may not support the same result, commentators describe the following seven factors as the most important:

- The degree of control exercised by the principal over the details of the work.

- Which party invests in the facilities used in the work?

- The opportunity of the worker for profit or loss.

- Whether the principal has a right to discharge the worker.

- Whether the work is part of the principal's regular business.

- The permanency of the relationship.

- The type of relationship that the principal and worker believe they are creating.

A quick check list of things you need as an independent consultant:

☐   EIN Employer Identification Number

☐   Business license (if your city, county or state requires it)

☐   Business bank account (checking or savings or both)

☐   Business card with business contact information

☐   Business letterhead with business contact information

☐   Health insurance

If you have any questions about whether or not you are an independent contractor, talk with your CPA or call the state. The state is interested in working with you to determine your status. They have a form (Determination of Employment Work Status for Purposes of State Employment Taxes and Personal Income Tax Withholding) which will help in the determination of whether you are operating as an independent contractor.

CHAPTER 9 GETTING PEOPLE'S MONEY

Your ability to accept credit cards can increase sales in a storefront business by 19 percent—without any additional promotions! For a mail order or Internet business, credit card purchases could be as high as 85-95 percent. When times are tough economically, more business is done on credit cards because the consumer does not have the cash. Studies show that consumers carry an average of $22 cash with them.

Think that accepting credit cards won't make much of a difference to your business? A Federal Reserve's Payment Study in 2007 found that two-thirds of payments in the United States are made up of cashless payments.

Accepting credit cards will cost you money. When you sign a contract with a merchant bank, you are taking on additional responsibilities, compliance, and regulations.

This chapter is designed to allow you to compare apples with apples. We want you to know what to expect, to become an informed merchant when you apply for merchant status.

Let's compare merchant status to something you already know—your checking account.

Let's say that you are a business and accepted your first customer's check. Yippee, you're rich! Not so quick there partner, a check is nice but how are you going to turn that into something you can spend (cash). You can't go to the grocery store and say here's my customer's check, I'd like to trade it for food. Although some stores may do that (it's called cashing a two-party check) it's not easy.

Similarly with a merchant status, when a customer gives you their credit card number, how do you get the money out of the little plastic card and into your bank account? You have to first apply with a merchant bank to accept customer's credit cards (merchant status).

SHOPPING CART

"Can't I just have a shopping cart?" Whoa there partner! This is not magic, just mechanics. It's now simpler, and many of these steps are provided by a single company!

A word of caution: not all merchant banks work with all shopping carts system. Duh you say, this doesn't make sense. Yes and no. What you may think is universal isn't. The merchant banks have their own banking software. To get that software to mate with all the Web software that developers create ain't easy. So before you sign up or buy something that you like, double check with your merchant bank that they can make the connection.

Many of the Web site development software packages will allow you to create a simple shopping cart and integrate it into your Web site. For the best results, choose shopping cart software that is specifically designed for the purpose and integrate it into your Web site's design. BUT FIRST YOU NEED MERCHANT STATUS.

Several products that work well at low cost are:

- www.PayPal.com for products and services (free until a purchase is made)

- www.PayLoadz.com for downloadable products (free until a purchase is made)

- www.1and1.com e-commerce site for $10 a month includes Web site development software

- www.ShopFactory.com shopping cart software $39.95-$64.95 per month or $499 to $999 to purchase.

FEES

The first thing that you would do to open a checking account would be to find a bank. It's the same thing with a merchant status, except we call them merchant banks. These are banks that handle your merchant account.

With your checking account, when you created the account, the banker informed you about the fees. Such as the ATM fee, the calling up the bank fee, the talking to a live person fee, etc. Same thing with a merchant status, there are numerous fees like the discount rate (which is different for MasterCard and Visa), there is a fee if you do not physically swipe the card, or if the card is an International card. There are more fees, so review all the possible fees.

Discount Rate

Checking account: the discount rate is more like when you are looking for a mortgage and they add on the points to the loan, that's the bank fee.

Merchant status: For every $100 the customer spends using a credit card, only $97 goes into your bank account because there is a three percent discount rate. The discount rate is a percentage of the total sales that is kept by the merchant bank.

The discount rate varies. Two percent to seven percent is normal for retail stores and some mail order businesses. Seven percent to 12 percent is typical for newly formed mail order and Internet companies. Outbound telemarketing in the adult entertainment industry and Internet business could have a discount rate as high as 35 percent. Other high-risk industries are travel, vitamins, or those with membership sales (automatic renewal membership).

Swap meets, fairs, and trade shows have their own hazards. Because these types of events frequently do not have telephone lines or electricity, a con artist can go from booth to booth making purchases, knowing that a stolen card would not be detected quickly. Equipment is available that uses a cell phone and a battery operated credit card machine to help process orders on site immediately, however the price tends to be high and not economically efficient for low volume or occasional use.

Monthly Minimum Volume

Checking account: when you open a checking account, the bank (or the type of account) may state that you must have a monthly balance of $1000. If you drop below that, the bank will charge you a fee.

Merchant status: The merchant bank may require a monthly minimum volume in credit card sales. This could be as low as 1¢. A common range is $200 to $400. The merchant bank will charge the account $5, $10, or $15 if the total monthly volume of credit card sales is below the minimum.

Transaction Fee

Checking account: you get several checks a day for orders and prepare a deposit slip to deposit the checks. Then you go to the ATM and make the deposit. To use the ATM, the bank may charge you a fee.

Merchant status: depositing your credit cards sales to your account is the transaction fee. Batches are typically prepared at the end of the day, after all transactions have been completed. Don't batch after each individual sale. Most systems now batch daily automatically. In the olden days, this was done manually. The transaction fee is 25¢ to 45¢.

A batch closure is the transaction that closes and initiates settlement at the end of each day. It's when the money from the customer's credit card is actually transferred to your bank account.

Statement Fee

Checking account: the bank charges a statement fee each month.

Merchant status: Many merchant banks now don't have a statement fee if you elect paperless statements. Otherwise, there is a $5 to $25 monthly statement fee. This is a couple of pieces of paper so that you can figure out what the actual discount rate of a transaction was, the transaction fee and any additional charges for the money, such as foreign currency exchange fee. If you obtain a merchant account from Costco's Executive Membership or Sam's Club Plus Membership, there is no monthly statement fee.

Reserve

Checking account: in addition to opening a checking account, the bank required that you open a savings account and have money in the savings account in case you wrote a check for more money than was in the checking account.

Merchant status: The merchant bank may require reserve funds, an escrow account, or could hold back a percentage of every sale for as long as 180 days, with low or no interest in order to build a reserve fund against possible chargebacks. This should be an option of last resort. If there is no other way that the merchant bank will grant you merchant status, we suggest establishing a reserve (as low as possible). As soon as you have established that you are a reputable, trustworthy business, have the reserve removed.

Some merchant banks require that you have an account (savings or checking) with that merchant bank when establishing a merchant status, although this is not typical. Some businesses use the required account as a holding place where the funds are deposited and then withdraw and deposit them into their operating account.

Funds Availability

Checking account: an in-state check, funds would be available in five business days, an out-of-state check ten business days.

Merchant status: Most merchant banks make the transfers within 24 to 48 hours. Anything longer than that is not a normal merchant banking procedure, so find another merchant bank. American Express tends to be a little slower—48 to 72 hours.

Setup Fee

There are some merchant banks that are charging a setup fee, which may cost you approximately $200. If your merchant bank charges a setup fee, try to negotiate around it. Ask specifically how this fee is different from the other fees being charged to you.

Chargebacks

Checking account: Oops, there wasn't enough money in the customer's checking account to pay for the item—the check bounces.

Merchant status: the customer's disputes the charges on their bill.

Have you ever received your credit card statement and discovered a charge you did not authorize? As the customer, we call the credit card company (bank) and inform them that we didn't make the charge.

The merchant bank then gives the merchant 30 days (check your contract for specifics) to prove to the merchant bank that the customer did place the order. If the merchant is unable to prove the charges, the merchant bank processes a chargeback.

Chargebacks are the debiting of the merchant account (that's your account/your money) by the merchant bank. Chargebacks are complicated. They can be handled in an effective manner without jeopardizing your merchant status. Maintenance of records is important so that a chargeback can be handled quickly.

Chargebacks can be issued against the merchant account for up to a year after the transaction has been entered (even as long as seven years). This makes a mockery of the requirement of state attorney generals and other regulatory agencies that the merchant specify the return privilege clearly.

Merchants are required to maintain original sales drafts for a period of three years. A cardholder is permitted to request a copy of a sale or credit draft within this time frame. This is known as a Retrieval Request.

Here is a sample of the letter we use when we have a retrieval request:

> Date: January 42, 1822
> To: Novus Services, Support Services Dept
> From: Nancy Miller
> Subject: Ticket Retrieval Request
>
> On Saturday, May 17, 1821, from 9 a.m. to 4 p.m., Mike Rounds conducted a seminar for the National Management Association at the Burbank Fire Department Training Center, at which time Mary Jane Smith authorized to her MasterCard the purchase of the book *Fishin' With a Net* for $30. She took her purchase with her. Please find attached a copy of the order form that she filled out.
>
> Thank you for your assistance and cooperation in this matter.
>
> cc: Mary Jane Smith
>
> Enclosure: copy of order form

If the merchant does not supply the requested sales draft, it will result in a debit to the merchant's checking account. This chargeback cannot be reversed.

Normal refunds and credits are not chargebacks. Don't make cash refunds for charges that were made on credit cards. Refund cash for cash, and credit card credit for credit card charges. A credit voucher is a document executed by a merchant documenting any refund or price adjustment.

In all your advertising and correspondence, suggest that if the customer ever has any problem, that he or she contact you first. Handle the problems in-house and do not get the merchant bank involved, if possible.

With chargebacks come fees. These can range from a set percentage to as high as $100 per chargeback. If your business has frequent and excessive chargebacks, you might be put on a warning list and you could lose your account.

The merchant bank can terminate you at any time, generally without notice, and there is no appeal procedure. Like the hot list of closed checking accounts of people who have written bad checks, the merchant bank immediately relays into the banking system the information that you were terminated. There is little recourse. If you are dependent upon a merchant status, consider having more than one account at a time to protect yourself.

Application Fee

Checking account: go to the bank and fill out their paper work, give them money to open the account. And in the really old days, there was a signature card that you would have to sign.

Consumer credit card: fill out one credit card application after another and then pay an annual membership fee (if required). You fill out as many applications as you can so you can fill your wallet with all those nifty plastic things—MasterCard, Visa, Discover, American Express and Diners. It doesn't cost anything except acceptance or rejection when you fill out the application.

Merchant status: the merchant bank treats this application more like giving you a loan than setting up a checking account. The fee for the application is to review whether you are a good credit risk for them. In the merchant bank's mind, even though the money is coming from the customer's credit card and going through the merchant bank, what if the customer doesn't pay their credit card bill? The merchant bank has already given you the money. That's why not every merchant bank will give you, a start-up, home-based, mail order, Internet business merchant status.

The application fee is from $25 to $750. We have seen a number of merchant banks that are waiving the application fee. Many flyers and ads say, "We do not turn anyone down," only to be told, ". . . except you and your business" after you have filled out their application and written a check for the application fee. Ask if the application fee is refundable. We are beginning to see a charge for an annual renewal or membership fee.

When you fill out the application, check the boxes for which credit cards you want to accept. Although the most popular are MasterCard and Visa, you should also accept American Express and Discover.

EQUIPMENT

The credit card terminal has a little computer inside with your merchant account number, and your checking account bank's routing number. The only piece of information missing is the customer's credit card number. You key in the card number and via the telephone line, the customer's credit card is debited by the merchant bank and the money goes into your checking account (or whichever account you have designated).

Merchant banks usually will not set up a merchant account based exclusively on a manual imprinter. A manual imprinter is an inexpensive tabletop, push-and-pull device for imprinting the merchant's account number and the customer's name and credit card number on the credit card slip. Typically, merchant banks require an electronic terminal and printer. A few merchant banks still allow manual transactions.

An imprint is an impression on a sales draft manually obtained from a card with an imprinter or the electronic equivalent obtained by swiping a card through a terminal which electronically prints a sales draft.

The electronic equipment has greatly reduced the risk for both merchant bank and merchant. With electronic equipment, there are no carbons that can be lost or stolen. There are no bulletins or hot lists (merchant warning bulletins that inform merchants of stolen card numbers) because all this information is instantaneous during the authorization call. There is no floor limit (a limit established for merchants who experience a high rate of fraud to protect both the merchant and the credit card company). There are no addition mistakes or pushing wrong numbers (well, almost none).

The electronic terminal is more expensive compared to the manual equipment. However the benefit is that it will pay for itself with a reduced discount rate.

Hand entered transactions (or keyed transactions) are when you have to key (punch) in the numbers by hand. With all mail order or Internet orders, since you don't physically have the card, you will be hand entering the credit card number and expiration date. With some Internet shopping carts, customers will be entering their credit card information from their keyboards.

The transaction is transmitted via standard telephone lines. The money is transferred from their credit card and deposited into your account.

It is possible to purchase a terminal for $395 and the printer for $350. The Tranz 300 Terminal starts at $250 (refurbished $125) and goes up. The Tranz 330 Terminal is $199 to purchase. The Verifone 250 Printer is $99.

If you would like to lease the equipment, you can do so. Leasing the equipment could be as low as $18.50 per month. A typical range is $15 to $50 per month. A lease might be a tax expense.

Here are a couple of questions to ask if you are considering leasing credit card equipment.

First, find out the exact length of the lease. Will it be for a few months or forever?

Is there a buy-out clause? When you make that last payment, do you owe more money or are your payments done? Do you own the equipment or do you have to turn the equipment back into the leasing company?

Used equipment is around if you look for it. Check garage sales, the Penny Savers, eBay, or want ads.

Your merchant bank will charge you a reprogramming fee on used equipment. This fee can equal the cost of new equipment. Sometimes, however, the merchant bank will reprogram the equipment for free.

These days, you may not need a dedicated terminal because it may be software, Internet based or through a shopping cart. The same principal applies; within the set up are your merchant account number and your checking account bank's routing number to where the funds will be deposited.

With each passing day, new merchant software is available. This is an area where you do not want to put the cart before the horse. Many merchant banks' systems do not support existing software. So, establish your merchant account first and then ask what software will work with their system.

Software can cost anywhere from $200 to $1200. For instance, ICVerify by Tellan is $349; PC Authorize by Tellan is $200; MacAuthor (software) is $349; Citibank software is free.

Several Internet sites have popped up that will support your merchant account. www.Charge.com Merchant Services, 4485 Stirling Rd Ste 108, Fort Lauderdale, FL

33314, 800-706-3724. We used www.Authorize.net which is an additional $20 per month. Call your merchant bank and ask who they work with.

This type of account uses a Web site you can access from any computer. You log in with your password—no equipment to carry around to trade shows or in your office.

PayPal Merchant Services

We have signed up to accept PayPal. We sold a few items on eBay and were surprised at the number of people wondering if we accepted PayPal. We already offered Visa, MasterCard, American Express, Discover, and personal checks.

Nancy's NAPO-LA (National Association of Professional Organizers—Los Angeles) chapter began accepting PayPal for dues and meeting fees.

There is no setup or monthly fees with PayPal. The discount fee is 1.9 to 2.9 percent + 30¢ per transaction. They accept international payments from 37 countries. You have to wait three to four business days for the funds to be transferred to your merchant bank account. Our experience has been that the funds are transferred faster than three days.

PayPal has a **face to face** (merchant) account. With this account, you put the MasterCard, Visa and American Express logos on your Web site. You process the credit card, rather than going thru PayPal. The fee is $30 per month.

If you already have a consumer PayPal account and now apply for a merchant account, because your social security number is the same, it will take an extra day for PayPal to get the authorization from you that you to make sure that you are the same person (consumer and vendor) and not using a stolen social security number or have incorrectly inputted the wrong number.

For the customer, the name recognition is invaluable. Almost everyone has heard of PayPal especially if they have purchased something with eBay. If the customer doesn't want to give you their credit card number, they don't have to. This is secured information with PayPal.

For the merchant, there is no application fee, no monthly minimums, no additional software or hardware to purchase, and no statement fee.

You can TALK to a person. After you sign-in to your account, at the bottom, click on Contact Us, on the right side look for Contact Us by phone or email (click on that). Then click on Call us. There will be a PIN number and PayPal's 800 number. You call the 800 number and enter your PIN number and that gives you access to a LIVE PERSON!

Another easy place to establish your merchant status is with your **Costco** or Sam's Club membership. Your membership must be at their highest level, then go to the customer service counter and ask for a merchant status application. They have twisted the arm of a merchant bank to provide a very good rate for their members.

However, as long as you use that merchant bank, you must maintain your club membership.

The total time it should take you to get established with a merchant account is from three weeks to three months. Give yourself enough time to get all the paperwork in and the processing done. It can be done more quickly.

A good ballpark figure to set up a merchant account is $1,000. If you shop for a great deal, you could pay about $500. Ask yourself: Will this increase my sales by that figure after the cost of the product and normal overhead costs?

DO'S AND DON'TS

You should not accept or process VISA and MasterCard sales for another business. This is known as *factoring*. Unless you are authorized and established for this type of transaction, it is illegal.

You cannot establish minimum or maximum amounts for credit card sales as a condition of accepting any card. The discount fee and other charges are a cost of doing business; the customer is not to be penalized.

We do see signs in stores that say "$_____ minimum credit card purchase." In such a case, you have three choices:

1. Report them to VISA and MasterCard, as the merchant is in violation of its contract.

2. Play with the merchant. Let him or her know that you know that the action is illegal, then make a purchase of less than $10.

3. Smile a knowing smile that you know what the merchant is doing is illegal and do nothing more.

Neither you nor your staff can encourage a customer to use one card over another because you, the merchant, have a lower discount rate (for instance a lower rate on VISA/MasterCard and a higher discount rate on American Express).

Customers spend more when there is a credit card display visible. Signage boosts sales because it helps customers determine their payment options. More than 70 percent of your customers will look for signage rather than ask which cards are accepted in a storefront business.

CHECKS

The United States is still primarily a checking society. You will have to accept checks. Yes, sometimes checks bounce. The more unique your product and the more the customer wants the product, the fewer bounced checks you will have.

If you do get bounced checks, follow up and try to collect your money. We call and notify our customer about a bounced check. Most of the time they will offer a solution. You can deposit a check more than twice. Find out the specifics at your bank.

We attended a seminar at which the Los Angeles County District Attorney explained their Bad Check Restitution Program. You might check with your county district attorney's office to see if they have something similar.

The program is easy. Here is a breakdown:

Checks that were received for merchandise, personal property, or services, are eligible. The check is eligible if it was processed through a bank at least once and was returned NSF (non-sufficient funds), account closed, refer to maker, or unable to locate. The check must have been passed within the county of the district attorney.

You must file within 120 days after the transaction date. The filing is a form of a dozen questions and can be mailed. For example, you will be asked what attempt you have made to notify the check writer by telephone or through the mail.

There is no fee for this program and if the money is collected, you get 100 percent of the amount. Call 800-842-0733 for further information.

CHAPTER 10 WHERE TO ADVERTISE

When you start your business, the place to invest your money is in advertising and inventory (in that order—as long as you know where to get the merchandise).

Below are different methods of advertising. Some cost lots of money, others trade time for money. Speed costs, so how fast do you want to go?

The best way to get people to your Web site is to use conventional advertising to get your URL in their hands so they can go directly to your site and place their orders. So here are some methods of advertising to drive people to your Web site.

E-MAIL MARKETING

Anyone who has e-mail knows about SPAM—that unwanted, unasked for e-mail about mortgages, drugs and watches. Although as the receiver, we find SPAM annoying, using e-mail may be an effect way to advertise your business:

- stay in touch with your customers
- for private sales
- sending a newsletter
- sending a customer letter
- to announce and promote an event
- for seasonal promotions
- for special invitations
- for holiday greetings
- as a coupon
- for new product information
- to celebrate an anniversary
- and many other things

One of the major factors when using e-mail is the CAN-SPAM 2003 requirements. The requirements that affect you as a mailer are:

1. You must have an unsubscribe or opt-out link and/or instructions for the person to get off your list if they want to.

2. You must handle all unsubscribe requests within 10 days of the request.

3. There must be a legitimate *from* address, *domain name*, and *IP address*. Do not be sneaky about this.

4.   Have an accurate *subject* line.

5.   In your e-mail, you must have a physical address.

What the industry is looking for is *permission based* e-mails. In other words, the recipients should have asked to receive e-mails from you. That sounds great in Washington DC. Here in the real world, people forget that they signed up or registered with you. One of the ways to help people remember is to touch base with them on a regular basis. You don't want to burn out (over promote) your list.

If you want people to open your e-mail, here are a few things to avoid. Because the spammers use these frequently, systems use these to block e-mails, even when it is not sent by a spammer.

1.   ALL CAPITAL LETTERS. We explain this with *Easy to Read.* When sending out e-mails it is even more important to infrequently use all caps.

2.   Red text. Although it may look pretty, by using a large percentage of red text, you may have your e-mail blocked. This is an advertising piece and not an art piece.

3.   Words like *click here* and *free*, especially in all capital letters, need to be used sparingly. Yes, free is the most powerful word in advertising; however it may get your e-mail kicked.

4.   Excessive use of $$ and other symbols, and too much punctuation! Good grammar and spelling are important. Being creative is important. Use restraint when using symbols.

Starting out, you could use your little old e-mail software (Outlook and AOL). When you get about 200 e-mails addresses, you may need a system designed for the larger volume. Some of the current companies are www.infacta.com, www.ConstantContact.com, or www.IMakeNews.com.

The most important thing is to get the e-mail opened. Eighty-five percent of responses will be in the first 48 hours. Benefit driven subject lines with between 30-40 characters are best. The customer will decide in three seconds whether to read your e-mail or delete it. Test different subject lines to see which one pulls best.

The copy is important. Keep these ideas in mind:

1.   Less is more. Use one to three sentences when possible.

2.   Use appropriate graphics.

3.   Use white space.

4.   Check spelling and grammar.

5.   Incorporate a call to action. This is also called the click through. You can use more than one in your message (beginning, middle or end).

6.   Create urgency, such as a limited time, limited quantity, or a bonus ($10 off today only).

7. Write a headline that promises a specific benefit or result.

8. Grab the customers' interest in the first paragraph. If you don't, they will delete the e-mail rather than page down to read the rest.

9. Build value. People buy because what you are selling has more value than their money.

10. Sell your uniqueness. Explain how and why your produce and services offer more value.

11. Provide a guarantee.

12. Offer something for free—if they act now. Quoting the Shop.org/BizRate study, 79 percent of Web sites offer free shipping. Consumers state that free shipping is an important factor in determining where to buy.

13. Give testimonials.

14. Tell them how to order. Make it simple.

What makes an e-mail list so critical is not the mere collecting of e-mail addresses; it's the maintaining of the database. After you have sent out a campaign, your work begins with the cleaning of your list. You will get various e-mails back with different messages.

Bounced e-mails that are blocked, non-existent, or misspelled e-mail addresses. Take a quick look at the address and sometimes you can figure out the misspelling. For instance, EarthLink is a .net not a dot com. Current statistics are that there is a 30 percent turnover in e-mails each year.

Undeliverables, as the name says, are undeliverable. We have found that these addresses need to be double-checked. If we are using Constant Contact, we would send out the e-mail in ACT! just to double check. Sometimes they are delivered. We cannot explain it. No system you use will be 100 percent compatible with all ISPs.

Mailbox full messages do happen. We will send a second e-mail to this address about 30 days later. If the mailbox full message still appears, then we assume this is an inactive account and we remove the e-mail from our database.

Vacation or auto replies are valid addresses. Depending on your system, these e-mails may show up as undeliverable.

Blocked e-mails are not receiving your message. Try sending them a message from your regular e-mail (Outlook or AOL). If it is still blocked, remove the e-mail from your database.

If you have a low click-through rate (e-mails being deleted without being read, or only the first *page* is read), rework your message. How is your call to action? Too strong, too weak? Change it and test. How is the copy? Is it benefit-oriented or are you just talking about yourself? Look at the offer, is it compelling enough?

Even though people are shopping online, they still like coupons. Allow your coupon or the e-mail to be forwarded to family and friends.

According to Elaine Floyd in her book *Marketing With Newsletters*, use these guidelines when designing coupons:

1. Place coupons to the outside edges of the page for easy removal (lower right-hand corner is best).

2. Track response by placing the coupon on the verso (back) page from the mailing label.

3. Include a graphic of the item offered for easy recognition.

4. Run a dashed-line border around the coupon.

5. Include an expiration date and any rules or exceptions.

6. Repeat your company name and, in small type, your address and phone number.

7. Place an icon of scissors near the top left-hand corner of the border.

8. Place the discount or offer in large type as the coupon's heading.

9. Make the coupon easy to remove by perforating around the edges (if your printing budget allows).

One of the best tools for creating subject lines, headlines, calls to action, and benefit statements is Headline Creator Pro software. Look for it in the back of the book.

Social Networks/Social Media

You may want to consider these new forums for possible advertising. Even though they are popular, doesn't mean that they are a good place to advertise. Does your customer hang out here in the first place? If they are hanging out, are they also buying? Investigate before you spend lots of money or time trying to make it work. Check out SocialMediaExaminer (www.SocialMediaExaminer.com) for all Social Media. Scan the information for what is relevant to you. I find that they tend to get *saley* but it is always at the bottom of their e-mails so I have learned to ignore the sales pitch after I decide whether to join the event of not.

Delicious (formerly del.icio.us, pronounced "delicious") is a social bookmarking Web service for storing, sharing, and discovering Web bookmarks. The site was founded in 2003 and acquired by Yahoo! in 2005. It has more than five million users and 150 million bookmarked URLs. Delicious has a "hotlist" on its home page and "popular" and "recent" pages, which help to make the Web site a conveyor of Internet memes and trends. www.Delicious.com

Digg (since 2004) is a social news Web site made for people to discover and share content from anywhere on the Internet, by submitting links and stories, and voting and commenting on submitted links and stories. Voting stories up and down is the site's cornerstone function, respectively called digging and burying. Many stories get submitted every day, but only the most Dugg stories appear on the front page. Digg's popularity has prompted the creation of other social networking sites with story submission and voting systems. www.Digg.com

Facebook (since 2004) is a free-access social networking. Users can join networks organized by city, workplace, school, and region to connect and interact with other people. People can also add friends and send them messages, and update their personal profiles to notify friends about themselves. www.Facebook.com Mari Smith seems to have good content and free webinars about using Facebook as a business tool. www.MariSmith.com

Friendster is an Internet social networking Web site out of Sydney. Friendster is focused on helping people meet new friends, stay in touch with old ones and sharing online content and media. The Web site is also used for dating and discovering new events, bands, **hobbies**, and more. Friendster has over 90 million registered users and over 61 million unique visitors a month globally. Over 90 percent of Friendster's traffic comes from Asia. The top 10 countries accessing Friendster, according to Alexa, as of May 7, 2009 are the Philippines, Indonesia, Malaysia, South Korea, the United States, Singapore, China, Japan, Saudi Arabia and India. www.Friendster.com

LinkedIn (since 2003) is a business-oriented social networking site mainly used for professional networking. As of May 2009, it had more than 40 million registered users, spanning 170 industries. www.LinkedIn.com Lewis Howes seems to have good content about using LinkedIn as a business tool. www.LewisHowes.com

MySpace (since 2003) is a social networking Web site with an interactive, user-submitted network of friends, personal profiles, blogs, groups, photos, music, and videos for teenagers and adults internationally. MySpace became the most popular social networking site in the United States in June of 2006. MySpace had **layoffs** June 2009. The 100 millionth account was created on August 9, 2006, in the Netherlands. www.MySpace.com

Plaxo is an online address book and social networking service. Plaxo plug-in supports major address books including Outlook/Outlook Express, Mozilla Thunderbird, and Mac OS X's Address Book, though other ones can be supported through an application programming interface. Additionally, Plaxo can also be maintained through an online version. www.Plaxo.com

StumbleUpon (since 2007) is an Internet community that allows its users to discover and rate Web pages, photos, and videos. It is a personalized recommendation engine which uses peer and social-networking principles. www.StumbleUpon.com

Twitter (since 2006) is a free social networking and micro-blogging service that enables its users to send and read each others' updates, known as tweets. Tweets are text-based posts of up to 140 characters, displayed on the author's profile page and delivered to other users-known as followers-who have subscribed to them. Senders can restrict delivery to those in their circle of friends or, by default, allow open access. Users can send and receive tweets via the Twitter Web site, Short Message Service (SMS) or external applications. The service is free over the Internet, but using SMS may incur phone service provider fees. http://twitter.com

Other social networking Web sites are: www.Bebo.com; www.Classmates.com; www.Flickr.com; www.Orkut.com and www.Xanga.com. 360.yahoo.com closed in July 2009.

Special Interest Groups (SIGs)

With millions of people communicating on the Internet each day, special sites dedicated to individuals who share a common interest have appeared. Logically, if these groups are interested in the types of goods and services you offer, obtain a mailing list of the active participants; they constitute a targeted mailing list.

There are currently three types of SIGs:

List serve and related groups. The master index for these pen pal style groups is at www.Topica.com and will allow you to search for the types of interests that relate to your product or service.

Usenet News Groups. The master index site at http://groups.google.com offers complete 20-year Usenet Archive with over 700 million messages. These are electronic bulletin boards for a myriad of topics that can be segmented and used as a targeted database.

Chat Rooms. Similar to a conference call except that the participants use a computer instead of a telephone, chat rooms are places where people like to get together in real time and share their common interests. The master index for thousands of them is at http://chatshack.net.

NEWSPAPERS

According to Jeff Hockings, 17 percent of Americans subscribe to a newspaper. Although newspapers are not as widespread as they used to be, newspapers can still be an effective way to advertise. A lot of wasted dollars have also been spent in newspaper advertising. Be sure that it is the right place for you to advertise.

Go to the library's reference section and ask for Bacon's Newspaper Directory, SRDS Business Publication Rates and Data, SRDS Newspaper Rates and Data (www.SRDS.com), or Burrelle's Media Directory (www.BurrellesLuce.com). They all have newspaper contact information. There are more than 1,800 newspapers in the United States and Canada. Nearly 6 in 10 adults in the top 50 United States markets read a daily newspaper, and another 10 percent read one on Sunday, according to the most *Competitive Media Index.*

Local newspapers are the local city newspaper. If you are working in a tight geographic area, then these may be appropriate for you. There are places where the newspaper is the lifeblood of the community.

A while ago, The Hutchinson Leader did a book review of Nancy's book, *Clutterology® Getting Rid of Clutter and Getting Organized.* The article started, "Nancy Miller, daughter of Mr. and Mrs. Leonard Miller of Hutchinson . . ." Now, that is a small town. When Nancy went back to visit a year after the review, people still remembered the article.

If you are designing an Internet business, advertising in one of the top six wired cities (largest percentage of computer-based individuals) is recommended. Use a two-step ad driving them to your Web site. The top six wired cities are: San Francisco, CA; Austin, TX; Seattle, WA; Washington, DC; Boston, MA; and San Jose, CA.

National newspapers are newspapers like the Wall Street Journal, USA Today, and anything else that appears nationally. Although we would all like to advertise in these newspapers, they are usually out of our budget and may not be that effective for us.

Supplements are add-ons to standard publications. For some people, supplements are great. You will have to test for yourself to determine if this is a viable option. One caution: if the publication is free, those reading it may only be able to afford it because it is free. In other words, they might not have money to spend on your product.

RADIO

Radio advertising looks good to people at first glance because radio has been with us for a long time and they are likely to stick around awhile longer. Advertising on music radio stations incurs high costs because they reach a large market. Most people listen to the radio when in the car. Advertisers on music radio tend to be large corporations with multiple locations. What is so unique about your product or service that people will write it down or remember the telephone number after getting out of the car?

On the other hand, radio talk formats are excellent for the start-up, home-based, mail order and Internet business. There are over 300 talk radio stations that will interview you via telephone—you do not have to travel. Joe Sabah (www.JoeSabah.com) has an excellent list of talk radio stations that do interviews via telephone.

Go to the library's reference section and ask the librarian for the directory with radio and television media. Broadcasting and Cable Yearbook (international) is the directory for finding radio stations and their formats.

CABLE

Contact the local cable station and ask about their requirements for PAT (Public Access Television). The station will put you in a classroom for several hours, and then take you into the studio to learn how to operate the lights, the camera, empty the trash can, and sweep the floor. After the required learning period, you can produce your own cable show.

You are an industry expert and can invite other industry experts to inform the public about events, trends, and important information. At the end of the program, your business name and address will be listed in the credits.

Producing the program is free and it is aired when time is available. You can purchase the copy of the program. Then *bicycle* (that is, taking the copy from one studio to another) the copy to another cable station that will air the program when time is available, and so on from station to station.

Go to your local library and ask the reference librarian for Broadcasting and Cable Yearbook (international) and Television and Cable Factbook (US and Canada) (www.TVCableFactbookOnline.com).

NEWSLETTERS

There are several newsletters on almost every subject. With the British Royals, there is a newsletter on royalty postcards, a review of new books featuring any of the Royals, and a newsletter from the Commerative Society. Newsletters are looking for articles or advertisers. As an industry expert, write about what you know—your business.

Many newsletters have a rate for business card size. Don't put your business card in that space. Your business card is not an ad.

Your reference librarian may have Howard Penn Hudson's Newsletter on Newsletters, or Oxbridge Directory of Newsletters (www.Oxbridge.com).

MAGAZINES

Magazines are a popular media for generating business. Magazine advertising can be an excellent venue for you.

Do you subscribe to a newspaper? If so, how long do you keep it? At best, newspapers get recycled within a week. How long do magazines stay around? Much longer than newspapers. The last time you went to the doctor, you could select from numerous magazines—dating back anywhere from six months to six years! How many back issues of The National Geographic do you think there are?

At the library, look for Bacon's Magazine Directory, Ulrich's Periodicals Directory (international) (www.UlrichsWeb.com), or the National Directory of Magazines by Deborah Striplin (Editor).

In general, magazines break down into three types:

Business magazines are magazines like *Forbes*, *Money*, and *Entrepreneur*.

Consumer magazines are magazines like *Better Homes and Gardens*, *Popular Mechanics*, and *Oprah* of general interest to the consumer.

Industry specific magazines are vertical and concern a certain industry. They target specific interests such as fishing rather than general ones such as sports in general. For example, two industry specific magazines that feature the British Royals are *Majesty* and *Royalty*. An ad in either of these publications is very reasonable.

Contact the editor of the magazine to find out their requirements and guidelines for article submission. Perhaps they will pay you for the article. Even if they do not pay, make sure that your name, your URL, e-mail, business name, and city are listed at the beginning or at the end of the article. Some magazines will exchange ad space for the article or give you their mailing list. Standard Rate and Data (SRDS) is a directory to locate this information.

To find which publication to place your ad in, go to the library's reference section and look for Standard Rate and Data. Standard Rate lists almost all the magazines in the United States.

This multivolume set of books lists advertising rates. By using the cross-reference indexes, it is possible to locate publications that cater to any kind of product or service. An obvious place to advertise a fishing lure, for instance, would be *Field and Stream Magazine* because we know that people who like to fish read it.

A secondary source could be *Popular Mechanics*. The marketers know from their research that it is an appropriate place to advertise because people who like to fish also read *Popular Mechanics*, so they run ads in both magazines.

When you find the appropriate magazine, write down the telephone number (or address) and call, write or go on-line to ask for a media kit. This will contain pertinent information about the publication such as reader demographics, editorial calendar, rate card (the advertising costs) and, frequently, a back issue of the magazine.

If you go directly to the magazine's Web site, there is only limited information for advertisers such as the phone number and e-mail address. The rate card and editorial calendar are not posted.

SPACE/DISPLAY ADS

The old axiom *a picture is worth a thousand* words still holds true. In today's marketplace, it's even more critical for two reasons:

1. The average American functions on a total working vocabulary of less than 700 words. Therefore, most people are unable to fully understand and comprehend what you are describing in words even though it is grammatically correct and complete.

2. People see what *they* think you are describing, not necessarily what you think you are describing. Whenever and wherever possible, use some form of picture to let people know as much as you can about the appearance and relative functionality of your product(s).

Space ads are measured from one column inch to multiple pages. They have fancy text, clip-art, illustrations, or photographs. Space ads usually cost three to ten times more than classified ads. The results may make the difference insignificant. If your ad deals with a product and you need to get people's attention, then a space ad with a picture or illustration will probably work far better than any classified ad.

When creating a space ad, it is necessary to have a typesetter, graphic artist, or desktop publishing person. The layout is what the buyer is going to see and bite on. Publications do have in-house resources. Listen to what they recommend. Listen to them, however in the end you are responsible for your own business.

CLASSIFIED ADS

Classified ads are text only, usually sold by the word, per issue, with a minimum number of words. A large variety of categories are available in which your ad may be placed.

There are some cautions to be observed when running classified ads:

1. Make sure your target market reads the publication.

2. Place your ads under or in the right heading.

3. Code your ads.

4. Run ads long enough for a valid test (three weeks average).

5. Change the ad if it looks like everybody else's.

6. Write good copy.

7. Study other ads in the publication. If an ad runs over and over again, it's a sure indication that it is selling products.

8. Test your ads. If you are convinced they have been placed correctly yet they are not doing well, try another ad style or different copy.

When designing a classified ad, begin with a lead-in or headline—a word or two that grabs the customer's attention. This is followed by a promise—some benefit the product offers. Then comes the description of the product itself. Finally, offer a guarantee and push for action. Make it easy for the customer to act.

If you would like to place a classified ad, you might want to go to www.CraigsList.com. They have become the place to go to for classified, much to the chagrin of newspapers.

TWO-STEP

In their book, *The Complete Guide to Self-Publishing 3rd Edition,* Tom and Marilyn Ross found that "Most mail order experts agree that **a small classified** will not usually be effective for items costing more than $10 if you ask directly for money. So, use the two-step approach and offer to send more details. When these inquiries are received, you shift to the direct-mail selling approach."

A two-step ad is an inexpensive way to overcome objections. It's a way to overcome a major problem called *money insufficiency.*

Let's use the example of fishing lures. We have these great fishing lures, but we know that in order to make money they must be sold for $20. Why should our customer spend $20 for a lure when the discount store has them for 89¢ each? Twenty dollars for a fishing lure is a lot of dough!

We know from experience that if we can talk to people and explain all the great benefits of having this lure, they will snap them up for $20. No problem. All this means is that we need enough space to put down everything that it takes to cover all the objections people have.

There are two generic types of advertising. One is called the *Mercedes ad*; the other is called the *Hemorrhoid ad.* You have seen Mercedes advertisements. They are big, wordy, take up a lot of space, and they are expensive: . . . imagine, the wind blowing through your hair, the burl wood dash . . . leather seats . . .

HEMORRHOIDS? If you have hemorrhoids, your eyes focus straight in on the ad. People respond best if what they are being offered is familiar and nonthreatening. What is familiar and nonthreatening in your life? If you have hemorrhoids, seeing the word grabs your attention and takes your money.

Here is how you create a two-step:

> Miracle breakthrough in fishing lures. Catch more fish or money back. For free information, visit www . . .

They write, click, or call for free information. You send the brochure that explains away all their objections. They send you cash, check, or a credit card number and you ship them the fishing lure (or they visit the Web site and order online).

On a two-step program, 14 percent to 40 percent of the inquires will buy the product. What is more important, by getting responses from individuals, we know they are interested in fishing. Congratulations! You have just started your prospect mailing list, which means that if they do not buy the fishing lure, they may buy fishing rods, fishing reels, and fishing trips. They are viable candidates for your catalog or other flyers on fishing products.

In order to effectively use the two-step process, become skilled in the area of headline copyrighting and category selection.

1. Determine as much as possible about the individuals buying the products. This is your target market.

2. Develop and print a full literature package. Don't be afraid to redo it a couple of times until it is right. This could be your Web site or a special section on your Web site.

3. Locate the magazines or newspapers that your target market is most likely to read. Test several publications until the best one is located.

4. Look at the most important benefit to the consumer and write a headline that draws people to it. Test several different headlines until the one that pulls the best is determined.

5. Develop a small space ad or classified ad around the headline that invites people to write for FREE information and place the ad in the publication(s). Do not forget to code the ads.

6. When the inquiries arrive, enter them in the database and send them the full literature package or send them to your Web site.

7. Keep track of the number of inquiries and where they came from. This should be done on a weekly basis. Cancel ads that do not pull.

8. Be sure to keep track of customer activity on a consistent and accurate basis. These people have shown an interest in the offerings.

One of the best tools for creating subject lines, headlines, calls to action, and benefit statements is Headline Creator Pro software. Look for it in the back of the book.

Build it and they will come works well in the movies. However, for a business, you need to advertise. There are many places to advertise. Some may work for you, others may not. There is no magic crystal ball to look into to see what will work. You have to test. Just because something is new, doesn't mean that it is going to be better. Test it out.

CHAPTER 11 ADVERTISING

Advertising—successful advertising, that is—is your doorway to profits. Properly done, ads can make you wealthy. Improperly done, they can be one of the biggest financial drains you have ever encountered.

There are many ways to conduct advertising research, including hiring a professional agency. Before you say, "I can't afford it," think carefully about whether or not you can afford to make mistakes in placing your ads yourself. Getting customers is like going fishing. All fish have to eat. If you are using the wrong bait (ad copy), they will bite on somebody else's bait because it is more appealing to them. Make sure your bait is the right bait and you will catch more customers. A book that is worth your time to read is *Do-It-Yourself Marketing* Research by George Edward Breen and Albert B. Blankenship.

Recently there was an ad in a trade association's magazine that we belonged to. The ad said:

The first rule of advertising is ADVERTISE!

Often times there is advertising in publications that are nothing more than someone's business card or a glorified résumé. An ad has specific elements. Those elements of an ad are:

- Begin with a lead-in or headline—a word or two that grabs the customer's attention

- This is followed by a promise—some benefit the product offers.

- The description of the product itself.

- Offer a guarantee, and push for action.

- Make it easy for the customer to act.

The most critical part of the ad process is writing good copy. In order to benefit fully from advertising, copy must be carefully prepared. The first step is to determine what the advertising copy is supposed to accomplish.

While creativity is obviously restricted by space limitation, there are several guidelines to adhere to in the preparation of copy for advertising.

Effective copy must combine simplicity with brevity. Don't get too tricky. Never be verbose. Make your point quickly. While there is no specified limit to the number of words, the copy should be concise enough to register quickly.

Effective advertising should follow these guidelines:

1. bold colors

2. few words

3. large illustrations

4. legible type

5. product identification

6. short copy

7. short words

8. simple background

A great ad placed in an inappropriate place will cost you money and net you nothing. The same ad, placed in a publication and in a manner where the greatest number of potential, qualified buyers will see it, is a minimal investment because of the returns it will bring.

POSTCARDS

Postcards are an often-overlooked method of using direct mail, both to build your own customer list and to drive prospects to your Web site. First-class postage for postcards is 28¢ compared to 44¢ for an envelope.

You can have 250 four-color postcards printed for $95. Contact Modern Postcard (800-959-8365 www.ModernPostcard.com).

We have recently been told about www.OverNightPrints.com. We have not yet used them, but a 4x6 postcard, minimum quantity of 25 is $4.95. They have increments of 25; 50; 100; 250; 500; and up. Free shipping over $150. Sounds like a good deal.

A minimum of three people will read a postcard. Postcards tend to be kept for a longer period of time, such as being posted on a bulletin board. Do you think that postcards don't work or get read? In a survey by the USPS, they reported the following items were read immediately:

76.1 percent postcards
74.3 percent letter size envelope
71.8 percent larger than letter size envelope
70.5 percent newspaper or magazine
67.6 percent flyer
67.1 percent catalog

On a direct mail envelope, the biggest obstacle is to get the envelope opened. Teaser copy on the envelope helps to increase the likelihood of getting the envelope opened. So do hand-written addresses. A stamp (rather than meter indicia) helps to increase the likelihood of the piece being opened, as does the stamp placed on the envelope slightly crooked angel.

Now, a reality check. Although all this information is true, you are dealing on a much smaller scale. For companies such as Sears or Lillian Vernon whose mailing lists are in the millions, that small percentage makes a huge difference.

We typically send out a mailing of a couple hundred pieces, perhaps a thousand. The small percentage difference is so insignificant that we don't waste our time on those techniques.

For years, people have said that if the envelope has a bulk stamp, people tend to toss it out. Based on Nancy's clutter seminars, people do not necessarily toss material with a bulk stamp. We first look and see if there is a bulk stamp and if there is, then we look at the return address. If we don't know whom the envelope is from, then we tend to toss it out.

A couple of years ago, we did a test of delivery efficiency. We mailed an envelope from our office to the same test location. We found that if we used a postage meter rather than a stamp, the envelope was delivered two days sooner. If we used a typed address rather than a hand-written address, the envelope was delivered two days sooner. If you find that people are not getting your mail in a timely fashion, look at how you are preparing the envelope. Getting a postage meter and typing the address could get the piece delivered up to four days sooner.

If you are mailing 200 pieces or more of the same piece, consider mailing it out bulk mail. There is a yearly permit for bulk mail (first time application fee plus $160 from January 1st to December 31st.) Contact your local Post Office and ask when they will be holding their bulk mail class. For a few hours of your time, they will teach you how to band and separate your mailing, what a ZIP code presort is, and so forth. Even if you never use bulk mail, the class gives you some insights into why the Post Office does some of the strange things it does.

A bit of trivia. ZIP is actually an acronym for *Zoning Improvement Plan* and there for should always be in CAPS.

There are many horror stories about bulk mail being delivered slowly or not at all. We have found that bulk mail within the seven counties near Los Angeles was delivered within two days, and in some locations, the next day. We have not experienced any horror stories personally.

With a bulk mailing, NIXIES (not deliverable) or FOE (forwarding order expired) has to be paid for each piece is the cost of first-class postage upon return to you. So if you are looking at cleaning your list, and a lot of people have moved, it could become expensive to use bulk mail with updated addresses.

Another way that you can look more businesslike is to use a postage meter for your outgoing mail. Postage meters have several advantages:

1. Each additional ounce is 17¢. Using regular postage stamps, you waste money on each additional ounce. When using a postal scale, a great method to check to see if the weight is correct is to put nine pennies on the scale. The scale should read one ounce exactly.

2. The Post Office generally handles meter mail faster since that mail doesn't have to go through the cancellation process of a stamp.

3. Meter mail looks more businesslike.

4. A meter can provide free advertising space.

5. When developing a mailing, consider using both sides of a piece of paper. Not only does it help the environment, it saves money. Four pieces of paper (normal weight) can be mailed for the 44¢ rate.

When using envelopes other than #10 (business size) and first-class postage, do not use a brown envelope. Use the green diamond envelopes. Postal employees see the brown envelopes and toss them into third class mail. If it is necessary to use a brown envelope, use first-class stickers on the front, back, and sides. That way, no matter what direction it ends up or where it lands in the mail pile, you will get what you paid for—first-class delivery.

MAILING LISTS

There are three groups of people in business. They are the unqualified individual, the prospect and the customer. Your results (number of sales) will be different for each group.

On an **unqualified** mailing list, the return (number of orders) typically will be ½ percent to two percent. That is considered good. In school, if you got two percent correct on a test, you would have failed. In the mail order business, two percent is considered successful—for an unqualified list. An unqualified list is an example of a rented mailing list.

If you do not have a mailing list, then it's likely that you will have to rent a list from a list management company or a list broker. A list broker prepares recommendations and serves the mailer by ferreting out lists that will hit the desired target market and produce high response rates, and thus produce profitable mailing campaigns. Brokers tend to be product- or niche-oriented (sweepstakes, catalogs).

When you contact a mailing list company, you will be renting a list, not buying it. You may rent the list for one-time use, two-time use, or even unlimited use. If you have rented a mailing list for one-time use, people who request more information become your prospects, go into your database, and you can mail or contact them as many times as you want. Those who do not contact you cannot be contacted again.

There are two different types of rented mailing lists: *compiled* and *response*.

A *compiled* list is like if you entered the data from the telephone book (name, address, and phone number or other source). Nothing specific is known about this list other than the commonality of a ZIP code.

A *response or reply* list is a list of people who have responded to an ad. In theory, a response list would be better for mailing than a compiled list. Test the list. Find out what your actual results are.

For e-mail marketing, three types of mailing lists are sold.

Random lists. These are lists where the recipient has NOT asked to be included in any mailings. Their e-mail got swallowed up in some sort of campaign and added to the list.

Opt-in lists. These are lists where the recipient has specifically requested to be included in offers of the type specified.

Double Opt-in lists. An example of this is a National Do Not Call Registry. To register, go to www.DoNotCall.gov and type in your residential phone number. You will receive an e-mail confirming that you have registered. You must reply to the e-mail, or you will not be put on the Do Not Call Registry. This is called a double opt-in method. A double opt-in list is the best type of list because people have made a conscious effort to join it. It was not an accident.

Mailing list companies often seed their mailing lists with several coded names to track whether or not you are using the list an additional unauthorized time. Typical cost of an unqualified mailing list is $50-$120 per thousand names.

Prospects are those individuals you know are interested in your product or service and have not yet purchased. The return rate is between 2 and 14 percent. Build your own prospects list. In the beginning, collect as many names as you can.

Customers already know you from prior business transactions, and it is typical to get an 8 to 42 percent return consistently on a customer list. Maintain your customer list. Don't let it grow cold and unused.

Hygiene is a mailing list industry term which means how clean the list is or how often it was cleaned. Statistics from the Post Office state that up to 20 percent of the people on a mailing list move each year. So it is important that the list be updated.

A well maintained list is worth its weight in gold. All those NIXIES (non deliverable), changed addresses, and address corrections need to be updated into your database. This can be time consuming. You might do well to hire a list maintenance service for this task.

Statistics from the Post Office state that 20 percent of a database will move each year. It's possible that in five years a database would be completely obsolete. Different databases have different characteristics. For instance, if you have a database of individuals over 60, they tend to move less frequently. College age individuals tend to move more frequently.

Another question you will want to ask is, "How often has the list been used?" *List burn* is when a list has been overused and instead of getting orders, you get complaints—REMOVE ME FROM YOUR LIST! NOW!

Addresses are usually supplied as labels. The names are available in different formats, such as Cheshire labels, pressure sensitive labels, or on a disk (ASCII). ASCII format is popular now with the ease of importing and exporting information. Cheshire labels are ungummed labels that are printed four across on continuous paper. Only a letter shop that has a Cheshire labeling machine can affix them. A letter shop is a service that does personalized printing, labeling, folding, sealing, sorting, and delivery to the appropriate transportation service. Pressure sensitive labels are gummed labels (peel and stick). They can be affixed by hand or by a Cheshire labeling machine. Avery labels are an example of pressure sensitive labels.

Don't be afraid to use mailing list companies. Mailing lists are their business. List companies guarantee that their lists are deliverables. For instance, here is infoUSA's Refund Guarantee:

"Our lists are compiled and verified to the best of our ability. However, we cannot guarantee the accuracy of the information furnished and are not liable for any loss caused by our lists or mailing labels. If you buy our mailing labels, we offer a generous refund guarantee, which is as follows:

If you purchase our mailing labels, we will refund 5¢ per piece for any undeliverable mail. If undeliverable mail exceeds 8 percent, we will refund 30¢ per piece over 8 percent. (There is no refund guarantee on prospects lists; 3x5 sales lead cards or diskettes.) Undeliverable mail pieces must be received by us within 60 days of invoice date.

Note: Postage refund guarantees do not apply to address corrections received by sender or street addressed mail that has been assigned a box in the same Post Office."

Lists can be purchased from firms like InfoUSA 800-981-2776 www.SalesLeadsUSA.com or www.InfoUSA.com. These firms supply highly targeted e-mail lists for your advertising campaigns and can be sorted by merchants, consumers, and other categories and groups.

Our local library provides access to InfoUSA through the library's Web site. You can even download the information. However, it may be useful to use a mailing list company and the sales people and have them walk you through the first couple of times until you get a feel for finding target lists.

In addition to including the standard information in your database (like name and address) input pertinent information about your customer: male/female, average dollar amount of purchase, purchase amount year to date, when last purchased, how people got on your list, what was purchased, how paid (cash or credit card). This additional information makes it easy to target offerings for additional sales.

Endorsements are a mailer's specific request for forwarding, return, or address correction. By applying the proper endorsement, mail carriers knows exactly how to handle the mail should it be undeliverable as addressed.

We clean our list with every mailing (whether individual or bulk) by using the endorsement **Return Service Requested**. The Post Office does not forward this piece and will return the entire mail piece with the new address or reason for non-delivery when you use first-class postage. This is a free service provided by the Post Office. For bulk rate, each returned piece would cost an additional first-class postage rate.

The Post Office reads the mail with an OCR machine. Do not put your return address too far down or the Post Office will consider the return address as your delivery address.

The Post Office is your friend! They have several free items that are helpful in designing your postcard or your direct marketing piece. They are: Notice 67; D-

1050251 Rev A, and the book *Designing Letter and Reply Mail*. Call your local Post Office **Marketing** Department for a copy.

By keeping track of what customers order, it's possible to create selective mailings to a small number of individuals rather than the whole mailing list. The day of the million piece mailings is gone. Utilizing database marketing, it is possible to target the mailing list with just what they want.

Describe your perfect customer. Just who are your customers? What are they like? Where do they live? What is their income level?

The more accurately you are able to define your perfect customer, the greater success you will have in selecting an advertising venue.

A friend of ours has a business that sells royal commemoratives. If she wants $2,000 to fix her BMW, to go to England, or just for a shopping spree, she mails out two-dozen price lists to her Victorians. These customers purchase Victorian collectibles. Like clockwork, she gets $2,000 worth of orders.

BEST TIME

Next you have to test to see if your advertising is effective. Although it is important for you to advertise, there are times when the customer is more receptive to your advertisement than other times.

When is the best time to mail an advertisement to your mail order customer? Here is a tip: the best mail order customers are located in cold, rural communities and Hawaii.

In the book *Direct Mail Magic a Practical Guide to Effective Direct Mail Advertising* by Charles Mallory, according to J. Schmid and Associates, Inc., a leading direct marketing firm, there are better times to mail than others. In descending order, the months are:

1. January	5. November	9. April
2. February	6. September	10. May
3. October	7. December	11. March
4. August	8. July	12. June

For business-to-business mailings, January and September are the best months. Avoid having mail arrive on Mondays or just after a holiday. The book *Direct Mail Magic a Practical Guide to Effective Direct Mail Advertising* states the best times to mail catalogs are September and October.

Consumers start to do their holiday shopping at the end of October. As the merchant, you had better have everything in place and/or mailed out so they have it in their hands when they want to do their holiday shopping.

If you are using e-mail to advertise, the best times to mail is when recipients are most likely to open their e-mail:

1. Tuesday	2. Wednesday	3. Thursday

The most likely time an e-mail will be opened is between 10 AM and 2 PM. Avoid holidays or long weekends and seasons like tax season.

DESIGNING ADS

Headline

Keep your headline to 11 words or fewer. Think about it this way: if you were driving down the highway at 55 miles per hour, could you read and understand the billboard you just passed? You have to grab people's attention; that's the job of the headline. An effective headline uses verbs.

The first ten words are more important than the next ten thousand! Some of these first ten words will be in the headline. They must be carefully chosen so they will cause the customer's eye to stop when it reaches your ad. You have only a second, more or less, to accomplish this feat, so your headline must have a basic emotional appeal. Use words which, even at a glance, penetrate the customers' subconscious and cause them to stop and consider. There are numerous words you can use in your headline to get the customers' attention.

When or where should headlines be used? In classified ads, in directories, in banner advertising, in e-zines, and in magazines just to name a few. In other words, almost everywhere.

Here are some award-winning headline ideas (according to the Journal of Advertising Research) to help you get your creative juices flowing:

Ask a question—offer an answer
- Are You Paying Too Many Taxes?
- Is Your Property Value Falling or Rising?

Arouse curiosity
- Ever Wonder How Your Cell Phone Finds You?
- Do You Know What Soda is Healthy for You?

Diametrically-opposed words
- How to Create Low-Cost High-Profit Products
- Simple Solutions to Complex Problems

Endorsement
- As Seen on TV
- 9 out of 10 dentist recommend

Facts or statistics
- 7 Habits of Highly Effective People
- 1,000 Places to See Before You Die

Familiar saying with a twist
- They Laughed When I Sat Down at the Piano, But When I Started to Play!
- They Laughed When I Started My Own Business
- They Laughed When I Decided To Teach My Children At Home

How to . . .
- How to Win Friends and Influence People
- How to Talk So Kids Will Listen and Listen So Kids Will Talk

News or information
- Recent News Events Show That Security Systems Reduce Burglaries
- Celebrities Are Losing Weight Using The Latest Fad Diet! Should You?

Quotation
- "I'll resign before I allow the old procedures to be reinstated"
- "That's my life you're writing about so please get it correct"

Shocking or emotional statement
- Running Presents a Serious Health Risk
- Boy's Life Saved by His Pet Gerbil

Testimonial
- "We tried several methods for removing the grease from our carpets but nothing worked like FeeboT, the wonder cleaner"
- "We shopped over two dozen stores and couldn't find a better price than at Feebo's"

We could write a whole book on the importance of testimonials. Whenever possible, include what others have said about you. Use testimonials because they are more credible than just plain advertising copy. If you say the same thing, it sounds like bragging. Get a mix of testimonials: male/female, large/small companies, local city/state, and national/international.

What is that, you say? You do not have any testimonials? Never fear. Quote yourself. What is it that you are saying about your business, your product? Add the quote marks and people feel it's legitimate. For instance, we used a postcard quoting Mike.
The most important part of the ad, a headline must stand out from the body copy. Keep the headline hard, fast, brief, and punchy. It should be in the largest font. One of the best ways to create headlines that work is Headline Creator Pro Suite.

If you are interested in purchase this item details are available in the back of this book.

Headline Creator Pro will automatically spit out time-tested, proven, result-oriented headlines based on the greatest headlines in history . . . and do it in 17 seconds flat with push-button ease.

The software is based on the pioneering advertising work of professionals like Victor Schaub who authored The 100 greatest headlines ever written and Richard Bayan who wrote Words that Sell.

The software asks you four questions about the product or services and then generates hundreds of headlines that you can cut and paste into your advertising copy

Sub-Head

Now that you caught the customer's attention (just for a moment), add a sub-head to the headline. The best suggestion we have for sub-heads is to study book titles. *The*

Self-Publishing Manual How to Write, Print and Sell Your Own Book by Dan Poynter or *Clutterology® Getting Rid of Clutter and Getting Organized* are titles with sub-titles.

The sub-head adds just a little more, or makes things a little clearer for the customer. The font should be smaller than the headline font however, not as small as the body text.

Easy To Read

Design your ad or Web site so that it is easy to read. For instance, capitalize only the first letter of a word. ALL CAPS ARE 3X HARDER TO READ. IF YOU HAVE LESS THAN 11 WORDS IN YOUR HEADLINE, YOU COULD USE ALL CAPS. WE SUGGEST USING BOTH UPPER AND LOWER CASE.

<u>Do not underline words in your copy</u>, for two reasons:

1. You will appear old-fashioned. Many of us learned to type on a typewriter. The only way to emphasize a word with a typewriter was to underline it. So, if you use underlining, you are dating yourself. What kind of impression do you want to make? What is the tone or slant, and would underlining compliment the tone?

2. An underlined word is associated with a hyperlink. Even if it is the printed word, people look at the underlined word and try to figure out the URL. www.RoundsMiller.com

Use bold or italics instead of underlining. You can even change fonts (stay within a font family) or size of a font for emphasis.

Use restraint. You cannot put everything in your ad. We know you are excited about your product. Pick one, maybe two, key points. People don't have time to read or listen to even the good stuff because they have so much to do.

Be generous in your use of white space. What is white space, you say? White space is not filling up every space with copy. Keep the font size a readable size (8+), and leave an appropriate margin on the top and bottom as well as the left and right side. Do not make your ad or Web site look like the small print of a contract! People know that the information is important (and usually legal). It is just too hard to read the small print.

Use a serif font, not a sans serif font. A serif font has little tails and hands that, when reading a word, help to hook the letters together to form the word. Here is an example of sans serif and a serif font:

This is a sample of a sans serif font, typically an Arial font.

This is a sample of a serif font, typically a Times New Roman font. This type reads 12 percent faster than sans serif.

Help the customer to keep reading from one section (the headline) to the next section (the sub-head) to the next section (body copy). There are several ways to ensure that the customer reads on.

Use an ellipse. You know these as the . . .. An ellipse is used when the quotation is intended to trail off and then pick up again on another part of the postcard or on the next page.

They all laughed . . .

. . . when I sat down to play the piano.

If we were to say, "Knock knock," you would reply, "Who's there?" without any prompting. Using the . . . the customer wants to complete the sentence, complete the thought, or figure it out.

The headline is the largest font. As the customer reads down the ad, decrease the font size. This is a subtle way of telling the customer what is most important, what is almost as important, what is important, and what is not so important.

If you remember your e-mail etiquette, sending a message in all upper case was like shouting. Designing an ad in all the same font is like shouting because the customer cannot figure out what is important and what is not.

SELL THE BENEFITS

You may have heard this before, *Sell the sizzle, not the steak.* That means sell the benefits, not the features. Is a coffee maker in a hotel room a feature or a benefit? For the longest time, although we understood the words, we did not understand the concept. Another way of saying it is, *which means . . .*

For example, a house has 14 bathrooms (the feature) **which means** that you will never have to wait to use the bathroom (the benefit).

Here is an exercise. On a piece of paper write down all the features of your product on the left-hand side on the paper. Add *which means* and then list one benefit of the features.

Now, write the ad with just the benefits. Sometimes you will have to say what the feature is. Sometimes you may want to use the transition phrase, *which means*, and sometimes you can use other transition phrases for variety. By using this method, you should be able to design a benefits-oriented ad.

SWIPE FILE

This is a collection of things you liked or did not like. When it's time to sit down to design and layout a new postcard, you don't have to start with a blank piece of paper. Go to your swipe file (also called an idea file) and let those creative juices flow. You are not swiping anything; you're just using the samples as a starting place to create your own idea. Search for interesting tips, facts, and jokes to put in your swipe file.

Your Exercise

Use this worksheet to think out your ad and to be certain you didn't leave out anything important.

What is your purpose for sending out this postcard? Introduce your business/service/product to potential customers. Explain in detail:

Who should be receiving this postcard?

_____

_____

What type of action do you want the person to take when he or she gets your postcard?

_____

_____

What kind of impression do you want to make? What is the tone or slant of this card?

_____

_____

What can you offer the customer as an incentive to try? What is the enticement? When does this expire?

_____

_____

What is your message?

_____

Include:
Name of company:
Name of product/service: Business phone:
Primary contact name: Business hours:
Business address: Business fax:
                                             Internet address:

REDUCING ADVERTISING COSTS

Here are several ways that you can reduce the cost of your advertising and stretch your advertising dollars. Some can be combined. Some will work some of the time. Not all will work all the time.

1. Ask for a cash discount. The first time you place an ad, payment will be made in cash (or check, which is considered cash). Cash discounts are typically between three to five percent.

2. When buying in volume (more than one insert), the publication may discount the cost. Multiples of three to six insertions are recommended. The reason you buy extra months is the lead-time it takes to get an ad placed. If the ad pulls well, you have more advertising scheduled right behind it. If you don't reserve the space, you will be waiting another two or three months for another closing date to get your ad placed.

3. One of the most successful rules of advertising is: if it doesn't pull, you pull it. Don't leave advertising running that's not pulling! Test your advertising. Do a 90-day spread. If it pulls, leave it. If it does not, pull it out and ask for credit or the balance of the money back.

4. After placing an ad for the first time, let the media representative know that you are interested in *remnant ad space*. Remnant ad space is space that has gone unsold just before going to press. Flip through a magazine, newspaper, or the yellow pages and spot the unsold space. Often times it is disguised as puzzles or games (which are a nonprofit generator for the publication), a full-page (or two) order form for the publication or numerous companies logos.

ADVERTISING CODING AND KEYING

If you were to go to your downtown and ask the merchants, "Do you advertise on cable?" some would say yes and some would say no. Ask those who say yes if they get customers by cable advertising, all will say yes.

Now ask, "Does the volume of sales from cable ads and their purchases equal the cost of advertising that way?" Few of those merchants will know the answer. All they know is that some new customers are a result of cable advertising.

So, is cable advertising bad? No, it's not. The important question is, "Is cable advertising effective for me?" That's why it is important to code everything—so you know what is effective and what is not. Stop doing what isn't effective!

The key is to test and keep records to make sure your advertising is working. The code is mainly to identify the source and success of a publication. If an ad is in the newspaper, how do you know the customer purchased because of the newspaper ad or because of your Goodyear blimp advertisement? Keep a list of the codes. Otherwise, after a few months you will forget.

There are several different types of advertising coding.

The most common code is in the return address. For example, PO Box 100 is your address. Add the code *A* [PO Box 100A]. Any orders or mail to 100A came from this source. Your Post Office is used to coding and does not pay any attention to the A. With a PO Box code, it's wise to talk to the postmaster or postal clerk to let him or her know what you are doing. You can use alpha or numeric coding. You can code a street address; 115 E Street can be coded as 115-A E Street. You can add a suite or department to the address: Suite 101 or Department A.

The best code is to misspell a word in the return address (for example Silver Spur is Silverspar or Silberspur; Rosecrans is Rosencran). This method does not add any additional expense to a classified ads word count.

If you are sending out literature with an order form, code by color. One time it may be brown, the next mailing may be yellow. When you get an order on brown, you can tell which mailing it came from. Color code can be used for year coding. A brown order form was mailed out in 2010, a yellow in 2011.

Many companies color-code their business reply envelopes in order to minimize their sorting time. Thus, new promotions may have a blue envelope while payments returned have a pink envelope.

An easy way to code an order form or flyer is to put a unique symbol on the paper. Then when the order comes in, you will be able to ascertain the source. Here are some typical symbols: ☑ ∞ ॐ.

When the customer will be responding by phone, here are some methods to code their call. Use a fictitious, gender-neutral name: Skylar, Robbie, Bobbie, Lynn, Lee, Billie, Chris, Frances, Joe, Carol, Sam, Blair. Then when your customer calls you and asks for Sam, you will know the ad came from cable advertising (or whatever the advertising code for Sam was).

An easy and effective code is to use a telephone extension, especially when you don't have any phone extensions. For instance, 800-757-7671 extension 11 is a code. When someone asks for this extension, you know they are responding to an ad that ran on, say, January 1 (11). February 5 is extension 25. This way, you can track how long it takes before the customer is ready to order after they see your ad.

Price is an effective code. Our books normally sell for $24.95. We have a special in the California School Employees Association guide and the price of *Clutterology® Getting Rid of Clutter and Getting Organized* is $15. Whenever we get a $15 order, we know where the order came from without the customer having to tell us.

Ad Placement

Now that you understand how people look at a publication, you can select the best place to put your ad in a publication.

In a publication that is read front to back (avid readers), the sought after location for an ad is called the **thumbprint**—the upper or lower right-hand corners. This is the most common location for readers to thumb through a publication. If your ad is placed there, customers will see it seconds longer than at any other place on the page.

If you are standing at the grocery store checkout and you pick up a publication, how do you read it? Usually by flipping through it back to front. If you are placing an ad in a magazine that is mostly skimmed, you want your ad towards the back on the left-hand side of the page where the skimmers will see it.

If you are placing an ad in a newsletter, the newsletter might not be opened immediately. In this case, you want your ad to be near the back mailing panel so that even unopened, it gets read.

If you are interested in more information on this topic, you may want to purchase Marketing with Postcards. Details are available in the back of this book.

We hope that Mechanics of Starting a Home-Based Business has been a source and resource for you to find legitimate information to start your own business or to provide you with an additional income.

There is a lot of information to digest. Pick an area that you think you would like. Don't just jump on an opportunity because *they say* it's the hottest new opportunity. How much time and effort do you want to spend? It could be the equivalent to another full-time job.

Business is ever changing. There will be new opportunities, new ideas and new cons popping up. If it seems too good to be true, it probably is.

Best of luck and may we see you out there in business.

Index

About the Authors

Nancy Miller comes from a home-based entrepreneurial family. Growing up, her father owned school buses; coin-operated laundries; the garbage business and dump; and the family was incorporated—all as a home-based business.

Nancy's practical, bottom-line approach to business is real world. She lectured on the British Royal family and sold royalty commemorative items exclusively by mail order. At any one time, Nancy operates several home-based businesses, including professional speaking, publishing, mail order, association management, and computer training, including a 2-million-dollar-per-annum computer firm.

Nancy, a seasoned veteran of the professional speaking industry, is an active member of the National Association of Professional Organizers; past president of the National Speakers Association/Greater Los Angeles Chapter and holder of their Golden Microphone Award for Speaking Excellence. She currently gives over 100 fee-paid presentations per year.

Mike Rounds is a dynamic, highly successful business consultant, author, speaker and trainer with over 30 years of experience in both the corporate and entrepreneurial fields.

His experience includes aerospace project management and the directorship of a Fortune 500 company and as an international project management consultant specializing in both new product development and marketing programs.

He has been an independent contractor since the early 1980s and continues as a consultant and professional speaker. Mike is known as the man who translates technology into human terms and his forte is taking complicated subjects and presenting them in a simple, easy-to-follow fashion and currently delivers over 150 paid speaking presentations each year.

If your home-based business fulfilling your GOALS for SUCCESS?

If not, a business coach can:
* Help keep you focused,

* Create a timeline to achieve the goals you desire, and

* Explore follow-through so that you achieve your goals.

As a past student, call for a FREE 30-minute telephone business coaching session by Nancy, a Certified Professional Coach to work with you on your goals.

For Nancy's or Mike's schedule, call 310-544-9502 Nancy@RoundsMiller.com or go to www.RoundsMiller.com for additional information, books and CDs, and additional resources.

PRODUCT CATALOG

Book Marketing for the Clueless®

Want to sell your books, CDs and DVDs for a profit? This audio/PDF CD includes databases of over 500 catalogs and outlets that market books and instructions on how to solicit your publications including how to be listed with Amazon.com for free.

Audio/Data CD⁺   ISBN 978-1-891440-49-6   **$24.95**

Cash From Your Clutter

A manual filled with resources to help you turn your excess stuff into cash. Includes information on what sells, where to sell your excess stuff, how to place a realistic sales value on your stuff, the best time to sell your stuff, how to donate for tax deductions, a special section on how to rent your timeshare property and much more.

Book   ISBN 978-1-891440-73-1   **$24.95**
eBook*   ISBN 978-1-891440-79-3   **$9.95**

The Clutter Bug Attacks Christmas Clutter™

If there's one time of the year our homes and lives become more cluttered, it's Christmas. Here are quick and easy ways to simplify Christmas, including how to: plan and organize your Christmas, get your card and gift lists under control, simplify your gift giving, handle the gifts you receive, and get rid of Christmas clutter!

Book   ISBN 978-1-891440-74-8   **$15.95**
eBook*   ISBN 978-1-891440-80-9   **$9.95**

The Clutter Bug Attacks Junk Mail, Spam and Telemarketers™

Overwhelmed by Junk Mail? Spam? Telemarketers? These can all be stopped! Current, verified information with visual examples for quick and easy understanding. The first book ever to show you how to get off of political mailings, plus proven and structured processes for both eliminating and retaining communications.

Book   ISBN 978-1-891440-75-5   **$24.95**
eBook*   ISBN 978-1-891440-81-6   **$9.95**

The Clutter Bug Investigates Coupons, Discounts, and Deals™

A complete manual describing the coupon process and how to use them to save 35 to 85 percent on your shopping. Includes complete detailed illustrations and examples on where to find coupons, types of coupons, store policies for coupons, deals and discounts, rebates and refunds, and rewards and loyalty cards.

Book   ISBN 978-1-891440-77-9   **$24.95**
eBook*   ISBN 978-1-891440-82-3   **$9.95**

Clutterology® Getting Rid of Clutter and Getting Organized!

4th Edition, Revised and Expanded! A complete manual on how to get organized, set up and maintain manageable filing systems, and eliminate clutter that gets in your way. Provides some of the simplest, easiest and most practical advice on how to remove the clutter from your life and get organized.

Book   ISBN 978-1-891440-62-5   **$34.95**
eBook*   ISBN 978-1-891440-71-7   **$9.95**

*eBooks contain a complete book in PDF for use on all Mac & Windows PCs, including desktops, notebooks/laptops, netbooks & tablets.
+All data files are in PDF format, playable/viewable on Windows and Mac, audio files are in Wave format playable on standard CD players.

Clutterology® Eliminate the Clutter in Your Life and Get Organized!

Companion to the Clutterology book, the information in this 3 DVD set will help you to adapt your home and work environment to your style and attitude. Recorded in-studio and contains a combination of lecture and actual demonstrations using dozens of common implements found in stores to organize, clean, and reduce clutter.

DVD   ISBN 978-1-891440-61-8   **$39.95**

Highlights of Clutterology®

This audio CD has over 60 minutes of tips, tricks, insights, and stories about getting rid of your clutter and getting organized. It's ideal for reinforcement to remind you that getting organized is a step-by-step process that you can accomplish if you take it easy and stick with it.

Audio CD⁺   ISBN 978-1-891440-50-2   **$19.95**

How to Become a Clutterologist™

Do label makers and shelf dividers make you smile? Use your aptitude for organization to change lives and turn your decluttering skills into a moneymaking career; become a professional organizer! Includes the tools and knowledge you need to succeed in the professional organizer industry: organizing specialties, understanding the Clutter-Hoarding Scale, how to structure your business for SUCCESS, business licensing and insurance.

Book   ISBN 978-1-891440-56-4   **$29.95**

eBook*   ISBN 978-1-891440-68-7   **$9.95**

Consulting for the Clueless®

In today's business climate, consultants are flourishing while others can't find a job. This book will show you how to profitably leverage your experience into a six-figure income with minimal investment. Includes DVD with consulting seminar, PDF copy of Marketing the One-Person Business ™, and support software.

Book and Windows Software DVD   **$39.95**

Contracts and Agreements for Inventors

Two dozen of the most utilized agreements to help ensure that what's yours stays yours. With the help of an attorney, they contain everything you'll need from a confidentiality agreement to work-for-hire agreements, assignment of rights, and partnership agreements. Comes with instructions for usage, filling out, and filing where applicable.

Data CD⁺   **$19.95**

E-Commerce for the Clueless®

A complete instruction program on CD that includes Flash® video on what E-commerce is and isn't, what's required to get involved, how to set up a web site page for e-commerce, setting up a FREE PayPal account and product purchase buttons, and how to set up a pay-per-download account to sell e-books and other information products directly from your web site. Includes royalty free background music clips.

Data CD⁺   ISBN 978-1-8911440-78-6   **$24.95**

E-Publishing for the Clueless®

Looking for information about how to create an eBook? Want to get your books and products on Amazon.com or listed as paid downloads on Kindle™ or the new iPAD™? Learn, step-by-step, how to create eBooks for literally *nothing*. Plus, how to publish a book with up to 64 pgs and a gloss cover for less than 50 cents per book!

Book and Windows Software CD⁺   ISBN 978-1-8911440-72-4   **$39.95**

eBook*   ISBN 978-1-8911440-83-0   **$9.95**

Fishin' With A Net

Learn the elements of designing a Web site that actually works for you and can be created in less than four hours. Covers what the Web really is, what to put on your site to be successful, and how to link with the search engines quickly and easily.

Book   ISBN 978-1-891440-55-7   **$24.95**

eBook*   ISBN 978-1-891440-42-7   **$9.95**

**eBooks contain a complete book in PDF for use on all Mac & Windows PCs, including desktops, notebooks/laptops, netbooks & tablets.*
+*All data files are in PDF format, playable/viewable on Windows and Mac, audio files are in Wave format playable on standard CD players.*

Headline Creator™ Pro Suite

"Your headline can result in 80 percent or more of the effectiveness of your ad or sales page!" Automatically generates time-tested, proven, results-oriented headlines based on the greatest headlines in history...and does it in 17 seconds!

Windows Software CD+   **$39.95**

How to Develop an Effective Web Site

Self-running CD takes you through the process of creating Web sites and getting them posted on the Web. Includes over 130 narrated slides with complete details and explanations on everything from renting a domain name cheaply to getting a shopping cart for FREE!

Data CD+   ISBN 978-1-891440-43-4   **$19.95**

How To Sell Your Inventions for Cash

Everything you need to know to be a successful inventor! Takes your idea from inception through the licensing process to a manufacturer for royalties. Learn how to protect your inventions using patents, trademarks, copyrights, and other legal instruments, determine if you're ready to offer your idea, and how to find and solicit manufacturers who are interested in your ideas.

Book   ISBN 978-1-891440-27-4   **$24.95**
*eBook**   ISBN 978-1-891440-69-4   **$9.95**
Audio CD+   ISBN 978-1-891440-28-1   **$39.95**

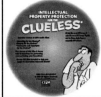

Intellectual Property Protection for the Clueless®

CD contains 3 hours of audio plus 100s of pages in PDF format on trademarks, patents and copyright. Includes forms for filing without an attorney! *Bonus: How to Apply for an Innovation Research Grant!* This audio is in MP3 format playable with the Windows Media Player or comparable MP3 software.

MP3 Audio/Data CD+   ISBN 978-1-891440-67-0   **$59.95**

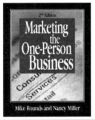

Marketing the One-Person Business

A one-person business is different from any other because you have to do the business PLUS get the business. Contains complete information about setup, operation, independent contractor criteria and forms, fee setting, consulting, public speaking, seminars, contracts and agreements.

Book   ISBN 978-1-891440-29-8   **$24.95**
*eBook**   ISBN 978-1-891440-41-0   **$9.95**

Marketing with Postcards

The most cost effective way to promote any product or service is with postcards. You'll learn how to design a GOOD marketing postcard that gets response, how to effectively evaluate your postcards before printing, and resources for low-cost postcard layout and printing.

DVD   ISBN 978-1-891440-34-2   **$39.95**

Mechanics of Starting a Home-Based Business

A home-based business is a business whose primary office is in the owner's home. Explains the realities of starting and operating a home business and including resources for taxes, licenses, and advertising plus computer operated business you can start and run.

Book   ISBN 978-1-891440-63-2   **$34.95**
*eBook**   ISBN 978-1-891440-70-0   **$9.95**

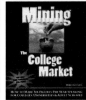

Mining the College Market

Local colleges provide hundreds of millions of dollars in revenues each year and are responsible for well over 200,000 paid training programs each year. Contains a 212 page manual with complete resources plus a three hour seminar on auto run CD, complete with narrative and slides plus a special edition of Self Publishing for the Clueless®.

Book and CD+   **$399.00**

---

eBooks contain a complete book in PDF for use on all Mac & Windows PCs, including desktops, notebooks/laptops, netbooks & tablets.
+*All data files are in PDF format, playable/viewable on Windows and Mac, audio files are in Wave format playable on standard CD players.*

Missing Tools Software Suite

Web site add-ons: Site search engine, Misspelling Generator that creates misspelled keywords to help overcome inability of searchers to correctly spell your meta-tags, Thumbnail Tool provides batch thumbnailing for images, and Slideshow Maker converts multiple views and turns still images into a self-running slide show presentation.

Windows Software CD$^+$ **$79.95**

Photo Manipulator Pro

Shrink Pic™ software automatically reduces the size of photos for email, blogging and web galleries. No set up, no operating instructions, just send your photos normally and Shrink Pic™ does the work. Paint Shop Pro™ 4 is an easy to use photo editing program that let's you enhance your photos and create professional-looking images.

Windows Software CD$^+$ **$19.95**

Professional Speaking for the Clueless®

Do you want to be paid to speak? Explains the REAL business of professional speaking and how to make six figures a year without huge marketing and advertising costs. Includes dozens of resources, databases, and complete explanations of how to locate speaking opportunities and market to them.

Audio/Data CD$^+$ ISBN 978-1-891440-53-3 **$24.95**

Profitable *PowerPoint*® Presentations

Turn your PowerPoint® presentations into profitable products YOU CAN SELL! All you need is PowerPoint® and a microphone - the CD has all the software and instructions to record, edit, and synchronize your audio and slides into an automated program; plus how to sell your products in class or as pay-per-download on the web.

Book and Windows Software CD$^+$ **$19.95**

Profitable Publishing for the Clueless®

The complete 3 CD set containing everything you need to know to generate, protect, and market your printed work. See full description for each item.

Disk 1 - Self-Publishing for the Clueless®
Disk 2 - Trademarks & Copyrights for the Clueless®
Disk 3 - Book Marketing for the Clueless®

Audio/Data CD$^+$ ISBN 978-1-891440-51-9 **$59.95**

Self-Publishing for the Clueless®

You can write and publish your own book for less than $3.00 per copy, in less than 90 days. Contains complete information, examples, and resources for everything you'll need including get bar codes, cover designs, and low-cost printing sources.

Audio/Data CD$^+$ ISBN 978-1-891440-36-6 **$24.95**

Trademarks & Copyrights for the Clueless®

Trademarks are the mark of your trade and Copyrights address the laws allowing you the rights to make copies of your work. Contains printable forms and examples, explaining how to protect your works plus what material of others you can use without fear of legal problems.

Audio/Data CD$^+$ ISBN 978-1-891440-30-4 **$24.95**

Venture Capital for the Clueless®

Venture Capital is available for all types of businesses and your ability to tap into it depends on your ability to write a business plan that sells you and your ideas to the people with the money. Includes explanations, samples, printable forms, and sources of venture funding.

Audio/Data CD$^+$ ISBN 978-1-891440-31-1 **$24.95**

---

eBooks contain a complete book in PDF for use on all Mac & Windows PCs, including desktops, notebooks/laptops, netbooks & tablets.
+All data files are in PDF format, playable/viewable on Windows and Mac, audio files are in Wave format playable on standard CD players.

VideoWeb Wizard™

Software suite to convert your audio and video recordings to Flash™ format for fast and efficient downloads of audio and video on your Web site. Includes VideoWeb Wizard™ software and tutorial, Flash Audio Wizard™, Audacity™ Audio Recording and Editing software plus bonus programs.

Windows Software CD **$99.95**

Whadda We Do NOW?™

Provides quick fixes for failing businesses. Learn how to quickly and easily figure out what's wrong so you can stop guessing and start implementing solutions. The information is practical, easy to understand, and readily implementable if you're serious about getting your business into a positive cash flow position-NOW!

Book   ISBN 978-1-891440-66-3   **$29.95**
eBook*   ISBN 978-1-891440-84-7   **$9.95**

Training Kits

Become a Professional Organizer

If you'd like to get into the lucrative world of professional organizing, then everything you'll need to setup a business, get clients, and operate profitably is on the list below. Contains:

Books: How to Become a Clutterologist™, Clutterology® Getting Rid of Clutter and Getting Organized! Mechanics of Starting a Home-Based Business, and Marketing the One-Person Business.

Plus DVD/CDs: Headline Creator™ Pro Suite, How to Develop an Effective Web Site, Marketing with Postcards, Profitable Publishing for the Clueless®, and Clutterology® Eliminate the Clutter in Your Life and Get Organized!

Kit   **$261.95**

Entrepreneurship

Do you dream of working for yourself? This kit includes everything for setting up a home based business, getting organized, raising venture capital to fund the efforts, scheduling and managing your time, and ways to market your skills profitably. Contains:

Books: Mechanics of Starting a Home-Based Business, Marketing the One-Person Business, Clutterology® Getting Rid of Clutter and Getting Organized! and How to Develop an Effective Web Site.

Plus DVD/CDs: Headline Creator™ Pro Suite, Marketing with Postcards, Professional Speaking for the Clueless®, Profitable Publishing for the Clueless®, and Venture Capital for the Clueless®.

Kit   **$169.95**

Invention Marketing

The material listed is endorsed by the SBA as "The only legitimate program for marketing inventions that we've ever seen." It explains how to organize and manage your invention process, protect them with patents, trademarks and copyrights, set up a home business, offer your ideas for sale, plus information for raising venture capital to fund your projects. Contains:

Books: How to Sell Your Inventions for Cash and Mechanics of Starting a Home-Based Business.

Plus DVD/CDs: How to Sell Your Inventions for Cash, Contracts and Agreements for Inventors, Venture Capital for the Clueless®, and Trademarks & Copyrights for the Clueless®.

Kit   **$161.95**

Professional Speaking

If you're interested in professional speaking, you'll find everything needed to get profitable bookings including places to get booked and instructions on how to do it! Includes over 1,700 pages of printable information, eight hours of video, four hours of audio, and hundreds of support resources. Contains:

Books: Mining the College Market (plus CDs), Marketing the One-Person Business, Mechanics of Starting A Home-Based Business, and Fishin' with a Net.

Plus DVD/CDs: Headline Creator™ Pro Suite, Marketing with Postcards, Professional Speaking for the Clueless®, and Profitable Publishing for the Clueless®.

Kit   **$461.95**

*eBooks contain a complete book in PDF for use on all Mac & Windows PCs, including desktops, notebooks/laptops, netbooks & tablets.
+All data files are in PDF format, playable/viewable on Windows and Mac, audio files are in Wave format playable on standard CD players.

Raising Venture Capital

Looking for money or backing for a new idea or enterprise? Confused about what to do and how to approach investors? We've assembled the materials needed to establish proprietary rights to your innovations; plan, budget, organize and schedule your project; prepare a business plan and shop it to people with investment capital. Contains:

Books: Clutterology® Getting Rid of Clutter and Getting Organized! and Mechanics of Starting a Home-Based Business.

Plus DVD/CDs: Trademarks & Copyrights for the Clueless®, Venture Capital for the Clueless®, Profitable Publishing for the Clueless®, Headline Creator™ Pro Suite, How to Develop an Effective Web Site, Marketing with Postcards, Clutterology® Eliminate the Clutter in Your Life and Get Organized!

Kit $191.95

Self-Publishing

You CAN have a book ready to sell in 30 days with these practical products...guaranteed! Contains everything needed including pre-configured scheduling and budgeting charts to get your own project finished in record time with a minimal amount of expense and hassles. Contains:

Books: Mechanics of Starting A Home-Based Business, and Fishin' With A Net.

Plus DVD/CDs: Self-Publishing for the Clueless®, Trademarks & Copyrights for the Clueless®, Book Marketing for the Clueless®, Headline Creator™ Pro Suite, and Marketing with Postcards.

Kit $261.95

Web Site Development Software Suite

No software you use to create your Web site will contain everything you need, so we've assembled the "stuff they left out." This suite of software and resources will help make your Web site work efficiently and get the response it deserves. These products have a proven track record in the world of Web design, marketing and advertising. Contains:

DVD/CDs: Video Web Wizard™, Flash Audio Web Wizard™, Headline Creator™ Pro Suite, Marketing With Postcards, Missing Tools Software Suite, and E-Commerce for the Clueless®.

Kit $100.00

eBooks contain a complete book in PDF for use on all Mac & Windows PCs, including desktops, notebooks/laptops, netbooks & tablets.
+*All data files are in PDF format, playable/viewable on Windows and Mac, audio files are in Wave format playable on standard CD players.*

6318 Ridgepath Court
Rancho Palos Verdes, CA 90275-3248
310.544.9502
www.RoundsMiller.com

Business, Technology and Organizing Training Specialists

ORDER FORM

ITEM (See Catalog for Full Description)	Format	Qty.	Price
Book Marketing for the Clueless®	Audio/Data CD $24.95		
Cash From Your Clutter	Book $24.95		
	eBook $9.95		
The Clutter Bug Attacks Christmas Clutter™	Book $15.95		
	eBook $9.95		
The Clutter Bug Attacks Junk Mail, Spam and Telemarketers™	Book $24.95		
	eBook $9.95		
The Clutter Bug Investigates Coupons, Discounts, and Deals™	Book $24.95		
	eBook $9.95		
Clutterology® Getting Rid of Clutter and Getting Organized!	Book $34.95		
	eBook $9.95		
Clutterology® Eliminate the Clutter in Your Life and Get Organized!	DVD $39.95		
Highlights of Clutterology®	Audio CD $19.95		
How to Become a Clutterologist™	Book $29.95		
	eBook $9.95		
Consulting for the Clueless®	Book/Software DVD $39.95		
Contracts and Agreements for Inventors	Data CD $19.95		
E-Commerce for the Clueless®	Data CD $24.95		
E-Publishing for the Clueless®	Book/Software CD $39.95		
	eBook $9.95		
Fishin' With A Net	Book $24.95		
	eBook $9.95		
Headline Creator™ Pro Suite	Software CD $39.95		
How to Develop an Effective Web Site	Data CD $19.95		
How To Sell Your Inventions for Cash	Book $24.95		
	eBook $9.95		
	Audio CD $39.95		
Intellectual Property Protection for the Clueless®	MP3 Audio/Data CD $59.95		
Marketing the One-Person Business	Book $24.95		
	eBook $9.95		
Marketing with Postcards	DVD $39.95		
Mechanics of Starting a Home-Based Business	Book $34.95		
	eBook $9.95		
Mining the College Market	Book and CD $399.00		
Missing Tools Software Suite	Software CD $79.95		
Photo Manipulator Software	Software CD $19.95		
Professional Speaking for the Clueless®	Audio/Data CD $24.95		
Profitable PowerPoint® Presentations	Book/Software CD $19.95		

	Page 1 Sub-Total	

Rev. 8-11

Profitable Publishing for the Clueless®	Audio/Data CD $59.95		
Self-Publishing for the Clueless®	Audio/Data CD $24.95		
Trademarks & Copyrights for the Clueless®	Audio/Data CD $24.95		
Venture Capital for the Clueless®	Audio/Data CD $24.95		
VideoWeb Wizard™	Software CD $99.95		
Whadda We Do NOW?™	Book $29.95		
	eBook $9.95		
TRAINING KITS			
Become a Professional Organizer	Kit $261.95		
Entrepreneurship	Kit $169.95		
Invention Marketing	Kit $161.95		
Marketing	Kit $191.95		
Professional Speaking	Kit $461.95		
Raising Venture Capital	Kit $191.95		
Self-Publishing	Kit $261.95		
Web Site Development Software Suite	Kit $100.00		

Amount from Page 1	
Sub-Total	
in CA add Sales Tax 9.75%	
Shipping	**$2.95**
Total	

Thank You!

Name (please print) _____

Mailing Address: _____

City, State, ZIP: _____

Tel: _____ e-Mail: _____

I authorize Rounds, Miller and Associates to charge my credit card for the items listed above

Credit Card Number: _____ exp. _____ CSS_____

Signature: _____ Date: _____

To Order By Mail:

Send completed order form and check payable to Rounds, Miller and Associates to

6318 Ridgepath Court

Rancho Palos Verdes, CA 90275

View our entire product line at www.RoundsMiller.com